COLIN REES

The SECRET LANGUAGE OF BIRDS

ART, NATURE & SYMBOLISM

With 246 illustrations

T&H

CONTENTS

INTRODUCTION

Man's feelings towards animals have always had the element of paradox, a mixture of fear, admiration, greed, cruelty and love.

Kenneth Clark, *Animals and Men*, 1977

This book has been a lifetime in the making. At ten years of age, I built a birdfeeder and acquired binoculars and a telescope. My days were spent observing and recording birds in the garden, the gently rolling lowland of the Vale of Glamorgan and along the exceptional coastline of South Wales. As my interest deepened, so did my appreciation of humankind's relationship with the avian world. Edward Armstrong's seminal book *The Folklore of Birds* (1958) appealed to my

love of history and social anthropology, and although I went on to become a conservation biologist, I have tried to sustain a wider outlook as a natural historian. The twelfth-century Welsh epic the *Mabinogion*, with its medieval folktales offering drama, romance and fantasy, was for me a demonstration of how people sought to acquire the powers of birds through metaphor and magic. Later, while living in North America and reading accounts of the history of Native Americans, I came to appreciate how animals, especially birds, are deeply embedded in these cultures – their beliefs, rituals, taboos and totems – and how their sacred animals were exploited for commercial gain by colonists.

Writing about the symbolism of birds has proved to be a humbling task because, as a scientist, entering the realms of folklore, ancient and medieval history, art, literature and music has offered a wider insight into the avian world. Many pleasurable moments emerged as I explored how deeply people's lives intersected and became entwined with those of birds. I investigated how the views of ancient cultures moulded our own beliefs about birds and witnessed how humankind often forged close utilitarian relationships with them. Artists developed creative techniques in appreciation of newly discovered habitats and the birds that occupied them. Poets and writers wielded their pens to use birds as allegory and later to portray an ever more distant natural world, while musicians sought to capture birdsong and imbue compositions with avian legend and folklore.

The rapid spread of technology and the increasing threat of climate change are slowly eroding our relationship with the natural environment. This exploration into the avian world offers a fresh perspective, and I hope the reader will continue to draw lessons from the often-wise sayings, fables, symbols and names inspired by birds, which – through living myth – infuse our imaginations.

Frans Snyders, *Concert of Birds*, 1629–30, oil on canvas.

Maker unknown, Native American (Tsimshian) raven rattle, nineteenth century, Skidegate, British Columbia, Canada, cedar, pebbles and polychrome.

BIRD INDEX

References are to page numbers for each bird entry. Common names are listed at the bottom of each page.

22

26

32

38

TEMPERATE & CONIFEROUS FOREST

44

48

52

56

44 . . . . EUROPEAN ROBIN
48 . . . . COMMON NIGHTINGALE
52 . . . . WRENS
56 . . . . BARN OWL

62

66

70

TROPICAL & SUBTROPICAL FOREST

74

72

72 . . . . LYREBIRDS 74 . . . . BIRDS-OF-PARADISE

78

84

88

92

78 . . . . PEACOCK
84 . . . . RESPLENDENT QUETZAL
88 . . . . PARROTS
92 . . . . TOUCANS

MOUNTAINS

98 . . . . GOLDEN EAGLE

106. . . . . COMMON RAVEN

110. . . . . PEREGRINE FALCON

114. . . . . ANDEAN CONDOR

120

122

126

130

136

GRASSLAND & SAVANNA

120. . . . . KIWIS
122. . . . . COMMON SWIFT
126. . . . . HORNBILLS
130. . . . . BARN SWALLOW
136. . . . . BEE-EATERS

138

142

146

150

138. . . . . HOUSE SPARROW

142. . . . . PHEASANTS

146. . . . . KAKAPO

150. . . . . EURASIAN HOOPOE

158

162

166

172

COAST & SHORELINE

158. . . . . ATLANTIC PUFFIN
162. . . . . COMMON LOON
166. . . . . GREAT CORMORANT
172. . . . . COMMON EIDER

182

178

WETLANDS

188

198

192

188. . . . . WHITE STORK 192. . . . . MUTE SWAN 198. . . . . CRANES

204

208

212

204 . . . . OSPREY 208 . . . . FLAMINGOS 212. . . . . AFRICAN SACRED IBIS

TEMPERATE & CONIFEROUS FOREST

WAXWINGS

FAMILY Bombycillidae

The elegance and beauty of the waxwing present a visual rhapsody, with a black mask over the eyes, waxy yellow along the tip of its tail, fine wispy crest and wings of warm cinnamon grey with dabs of red.

The Bohemian waxwing (*Bombycilla garrulus*) breeds in the northern coniferous forests of Eurasia and in western North America, where it meets the cedar waxwing (*Bombycilla cedrorum*). The demurer Japanese waxwing (*Bombycilla japonica*), with a black tail and red tip, is found in the Russian Far East, northeast China, Korea and Japan.

Perhaps unsurprisingly, given their exceptional colours and contrasts, across much of the world waxwings have been conferred with supernatural authority. In ancient Greece the Bohemian waxwing was associated with the goddess Aphrodite, evoking celestial messengers or representing metamorphosis and the pre-eminence of the spiritual realm. It was also linked to Dionysus, the Greek god of wine, appropriately since the waxwing can often be seen drinking fermented fruit. The Japanese waxwing is similarly revered as a messenger from the divine realm, its graceful flight and melodious songs seen as signs of spiritual guidance.

The flashes of red on the bird's wings are a particular source of fascination (one Inuit name for it, *tik-e-che-u-wuk*, translates as 'killer of

John James Audubon, '*Bombycilla cedrorum*' (Cedar Bird or Cedar Wax-wing, 1. Male 2. Female), no. 50, pl. 246, 1842, from *The Birds of America*, vol. IV.

Kiyohara Yukinobu, *Waxwings, Cherry Blossoms and Bamboo*, late seventeenth century, hanging scroll, ink and colour on silk.

small birds, as shown by clotted blood on the wings'). The Roman writer and naturalist Pliny reported that the waxwing's feathers were said to 'shine like flames' in the dark forests of Central Europe, while Gaius Julius Solinus, a Latin grammarian and geographer, claimed the Germans used captive birds to light their way when travelling by night. This belief prevailed until the end of the sixteenth century, when Italian ornithologist Ulysses Aldrovandi kept a waxwing in his house for three months, observing it through the night and noting that the bird stubbornly failed to emit flames or light of any kind. Scottish artist Archibald Thorburn perhaps best captured the distinctive wings, with tips the colour of red sealing wax, in his portrait of a Bohemian waxwing.

Across East Asia, the waxwing is held to embody auspicious qualities such as good fortune and joy, symbolizing beauty, companionship and harmony between individuals. In North America the cedar waxwing also played an important role in much Native American lore, with many tribes seeing them as symbols of peace, love and harmony with the natural world, and again believing them to be messengers from the spirit world or the ancestors. Other tribes held the waxwing to be a symbol of abundance and fertility, believing the birds to bring good luck and prosperity to all who saw them.

While the Celts regarded the Bohemian waxwing as a symbol of hope and rebirth, when it appeared in large numbers or 'invasions' it was considered a sign that something was about to happen – either good or bad. This reputation persisted in continental Europe, where the bird was accorded sinister associations and often foretold disaster. In some regions it was known as the 'death bird' or 'pestilence bird', because

Robert Greenhalf, *Waxwings*, *c.* 2018, woodcut.

Lucas Cranach the Elder, *Two Dead Bohemian Waxwings*, *c.* 1530, watercolour on paper.

Ohara Kōson, *Waxwing on Snow-Covered Branch*, 1900–30, woodcut.

when their northern breeding areas were in the grip of a particularly harsh winter, flocks of waxwings flew south in search of winter fruits. With a popular belief in the Middle Ages holding that plentiful berries in the autumn indicated a severe winter, the birds' arrival often heralded starvation, pestilence and death.

In the Netherlands the Bohemian waxwing is called *pestvogel*, meaning 'plague bird'. As the plague similarly occurred in an invasion-like manner, the two were connected, giving rise to a belief that the flocks' arrival signalled an outbreak of the disease. As late as the twentieth century, an invasion of waxwings in the winter of 1913–14 was later seen as an omen of the First World War, while an often-quoted couplet in Vladimir Nabokov's novel *Pale Fire* (1962) invokes the bird's sinister reputation to foreshadow the fate of a leading character:

I was the shadow of the waxwing slain
By the false azure in the window pane

It is no surprise that the waxwing's beautiful plumage has attracted many artists. Among them are the French seventeenth-century engraver François-Nicolas Martinet, whose male Bohemian waxwing strikes a somewhat unusual pose, and the famous French-American ornithologist and illustrator John James Audubon, who paints both male and female cedar waxwings perched together in a red cedar tree, the larger male shown above. Depictions of the Japanese waxwing were uncommon until the twentieth century, but a compelling woodblock print by the renowned artist Ohara Kōson captures its elegance. The two birds are depicted in sharp focus, set off by the tree's branches, which are printed in a way that mimics soft ink brushstrokes.

Renowned for their exotic appearance, mellifluous song, bouncing flight and dexterous ability to feed upside down, goldfinches are one of the most popular and recognizable birds on the feeder on both sides of the Atlantic, but it is the European species that has drawn the most attention, sometimes to its detriment.

The plumage of the European goldfinch (*Carduelis carduelis*) includes a red face, yellow wing bars, whitish rump and black and white on the head. By contrast, the male of its counterpart the American goldfinch (*Spinus tristis*) sports a striking jet-black cap and wings and gold body, though only during the breeding season: it is the only bird in the *Carduelinae* subfamily to undergo a complete moult, with the male a vibrant yellow in the summer and an olive colour in the winter.

The European goldfinch plays a significant role in the Christian tradition, which held that the bird plucked a thorn from Christ's head when he was on the Cross and it was splashed by his blood, resulting in the red spots on its cheeks. It appears frequently in Renaissance art to foreshadow the Crucifixion, notably in a *Madonna and Child* by Leonardo da Vinci (*c.* 1490) and in Raphael's *Madonna of the Goldfinch* (*c.* 1505–6), in which the young

Raphael, *Madonna of the Goldfinch* (detail), *c.* 1505–6, oil on panel.

John Siferwas and others, a 'Grene finch' (misidentified goldfinch), *c.* 1399–1407, from the Sherborne Missal.

John the Baptist offers the bird to the Christ Child as a warning of his death. In another *Madonna and Child* (1512–17), by the Italian artist Cima da Conegliano, a goldfinch flutters within the Christ Child's hand.

In the Middle Ages the European goldfinch was one of several candidates for identification with the mythical *Charadrius* ('yellowish bird'). This legend, which originated in ancient Rome, suggested it was possible to heal the sick by staring into the bird's eyes. By incorporating goldfinches into their paintings, artists were invoking the curative powers of the *Charadrius*. At the time of the Black Death, in the second quarter of the fourteenth century, the goldfinch's roles as symbol of the Passion and healer of the sick merged and it was considered a 'saviour' bird, often pictured in opposition to the common fly, representing sin and disease. To reinforce the connection, its voracious appetite for the Mediterranean holy thistle (*Cnicus benedictus*), also associated with the Passion, led to a belief that the plant endowed the goldfinch with powers of defence against pestilence. The association lingered, and in his book *The Art of Distillation* (1651) the English physician John French wrote of the bird that 'The flesh if it be fat is a great restorative in consumptions'.

One of the earliest known illustrations of a European goldfinch appears as a miniature in the Psalter of Robert de Lisle (*c.* 1300). Another features later in the Sherborne Missal (*c.* 1400), though it is misidentified as a 'grene finch'; this passable attempt to capture the bird represents its colours well, but not its posture. Perhaps the first reference to the bird in English literature is found in Chaucer's *Canterbury Tales* of the late 1300s, to describe an apprentice in 'The Cook's Tale': 'Gaillard he was in the goldfynche in the shawe' (Gaily dressed he was as is a goldfinch

in the woods). Later, the Victorian poets Robert Browning and Christina Rossetti evoked the goldfinch as a harbinger of hope and renewal.

Pliny associated the bird with fertility, and the presence of a giant goldfinch in Hieronymus Bosch's fantastical triptych *The Garden of Earthly Delights* (1490–1510), next to a naked couple, may well be a reference to the bird's fecundity. This is also reflected in

❈ François Nicolas Martinet, '*Carduelis carduelis*' (European Goldfinch), pl. 4, 1765, from *Histoire Naturelle des Oiseaux* by Louis-Jean-Marie Daubenton.

❋ Hieronymus Bosch, *The Garden of Earthly Delights* (detail), *c.* 1490–1510, triptych, oil on oak panels.

*

a Valentine's Day tradition, which states that if the first bird a girl sees on that day is a goldfinch, she will have a wealthy marriage. The promise finds resonance in an early nineteenth-century version of the popular rhyme *The Marriage of Cock Robin and Jenny Wren*: 'Who gives this maid away? / "I do," says the goldfinch / "And her fortune I will pay."'

The American goldfinch held equal cultural significance for many Native Americans, and in Iroquois folklore a goldfinch flying across your path is a reminder to live your life in celebration. One story tells of a flock of small, plain birds who ask a fox to make them appear golden bright like the sun. Pressing some colour from nearby yellow flowers, the fox begins to paint them with the tip of his tail. The delighted birds fly off before the fox can finish painting, and so to this day the American goldfinch is yellow like the sun but has 'unpainted' black wings and tail and seldom finishes its song.

John James Audubon rendered the American goldfinch in his inimitable style, with male and female specimens plucking seeds from thistles; one thistle bends with the weight of the upside-down male, who feeds with his tail fanned to counteract the swaying. He found the bird's song particularly attractive, writing in his *Ornithological Biography* (1832) that: 'So much does the song of our Goldfinch resemble that of the European species, that while in France and England, I have frequently thought...that they were the notes of our bird which I heard.'

Sadly, celebration of its whimsical song cost the European goldfinch dearly, as it became a popular form of home entertainment as a caged bird. Many people were uneasy over such caging. Audubon wrote of the 'distressing occupation' of performing tricks, 'doomed to toil through a life of solitary grief, separated from its companions, wantoning on the wildflowers, and procuring food in the manner in which nature has taught them'. Carel Fabritius's famous painting *The Goldfinch* (1654) depicts a chained European goldfinch, interpreted by many as a symbol of captive love. The artist completed the work six years after the Dutch United Provinces gained independence from Spain and may have expected his audience to contemplate it as an allegory of freedom denied.

In the British Isles several poets expressed sympathy for the birds' entrapment. In his memorable poem 'The Caged Goldfinch' (1917), Thomas Hardy raged at the plight of a weakened, entrapped creature, communicating a sense of rage at lost freedom and imploring that wildlife should not be seen as a possession or an adornment. Only in the mid-twentieth century did the practice cease.

Carel Fabritius, *The Goldfinch* (detail), 1654, oil on panel.

C FABRITIVS 1654

The dove, especially in white plumage, is held up across the world as a symbol of love, fidelity, devotion and peace. In contrast, the pigeon – though essentially the same bird – is often taken as a pest, unclean and greedy, despite serving as a valuable source of sustenance through the ages.

There are over 300 species of pigeons and doves in the family *Columbidae*; the most famous, the domestic pigeon (*Columba livia domestica*), is a subspecies derived from the wild rock dove or rock pigeon (*Columba livia*). For English speakers, the smaller species of the family tend to be called 'doves' and the larger ones 'pigeons', but scientifically there is no distinction. Along with the jungle fowl or chicken, the pigeon is the world's oldest domesticated bird, possibly having been bred in captivity in the Fertile Crescent for more than 10,000 years. It is found in ancient Egyptian hieroglyphics some 5,000 years old and was popular as animal-shaped containers dating from around 3100 BCE, as seen in a red breccia vessel in the shape of a pigeon. Documents from ancient Rome show that the practice of domestication continued there, with descriptions of dovecotes containing more than 5,000 individuals.

In Greek and Roman mythology, the nymph Peristera was transformed into a dove (*peristera* meaning 'dove' in Greek). The bird was sacred to Aphrodite, goddess of love in its many forms, whether pure or lustful, and the connection led to an enduring identification of doves with affection (for instance, in the phrase 'lovey-dovey') and sexual pleasure (reinforced by the birds' conspicuous 'love-making' during

John Tarantino, *Crock*, *c.* 1940, watercolour, coloured pencil and graphite on paperboard.

Henri Matisse, *The Birds*, 1947, collage.

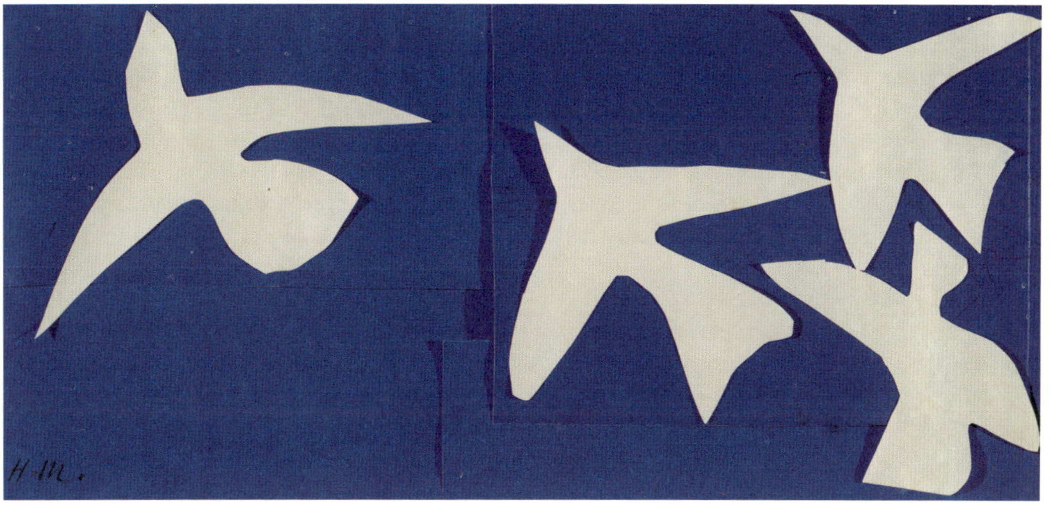

✳

courtship ceremonies). In a suggestive metaphor for a loved one, the biblical Song of Solomon implores: 'O my dove, in the clefts of the rock, In the secret places of the cliff, Let me see your face'. Such was the strength of these associations that both the Greeks and the Romans used dove's blood (especially from white varieties) in love potions. The practice continued into the Middle Ages with the inclusion of the bird's heart.

Pigeons enjoy a similar reputation: the fidelity of the domestic pigeon was legendary and a bird that lost its partner was said never to mate again. Aristotle praised pigeons' affectionate nature, and they became a favoured lover's gift, both for their erotic associations and as a symbol of conjugal affection and chastity. Conversely, the Roman poet Catullus advised that those seeking potency should avoid the consumption of pigeon: 'Ringed doves make a man's loins slow and dull: / Who would be lusty should not eat the bird' (Poem 16).

Elsewhere, the pigeon was credited with medicinal properties, its flesh, blood, dung and feathers being used to treat poisoning and other common ailments. The belief in such curative qualities may have arisen from the fact that the bird has no gallbladder and was therefore thought not to secrete the black bile associated with the irritable passions of humankind. In the Torah and Old Testament, the book of Leviticus offers instruction on how to sacrifice pigeons to cure skin disease. Live pigeons were once placed at the foot of a dying person to attract the pain.

In Christianity, perhaps the most famous mention of the bird appears in the book of Genesis (8:6–12), when Noah twice releases a dove (or a pigeon) from the ark to determine to what extent the floodwaters have receded. While the first bird does not reappear, the second returns to the ark with a fresh olive leaf in its beak, signifying that it has found land. This narrative echoes even earlier writings, such as the Sumerian Epic of Gilgamesh, which also tells of a great flood and a pigeon playing the role of messenger. In the New Testament

(Matthew 3:16–17), the dove appears at Christ's baptism to symbolize the Holy Ghost.

The image of a dove holding an olive leaf in its beak originally derived from ancient Greece and Rome and was incorporated into early Christian funerary art to represent the soul at peace (rather than civic peace). It appears in medieval illuminated manuscripts, such as the Hebrew Golden Haggadah (*c.* 1320–30) and the Christian Holkham Bible (*c.* 1330), showing the dove returning to Noah, while later depictions assumed a romantic quality, as seen in *The Return of the Dove to the Ark* (1851) by Pre-Raphaelite artist John Everett Millais, in which two of Noah's daughters-in-law nurture the returning bird. The image remains an iconic symbol of peace to this day, used, for example, in the logo of the World Peace Council, designed by Pablo Picasso.

In Japanese mythology, the dove is the familiar spirit of Hachiman, a divinity of archery and war incorporating elements from both Shinto and Buddhism. As such, it is seen as a messenger of war rather than a symbol of peace. One story tells of the hero Yoritomo who, hiding from his enemies in a tree, is saved from discovery when two doves fly out of the tree, convincing his pursuers that no one could be inside. Later, Yoritomo set up shrines to the god of war, on which were depicted the birds that had saved him.

Pigeons are held in high regard in Islamic traditions as they are believed to have helped the Prophet Muhammad on his great Hijra (the journey from Mecca to Medina). When he sought refuge in the cave of Thaw'r, a pair of pigeons built a nest and laid eggs at the cave's entrance, while a spider wove cobwebs across it. On finding both undisturbed, Muhammad's

✻

enemies were fooled into thinking he could not be in the cave, allowing him to escape.

The homing abilities of the pigeon have been recognized and exploited since ancient times. Phoenician sailors harnessed their navigational skills as 'living compasses', while the Greeks used pigeons as messengers to convey news from the battlefield and results of the Olympic Games, and as decoys (cruelly blinding them to prevent their flying away). The role as messenger continued for centuries, beautifully illustrated in a mid-eighteenth-century painting by the German artist Johann Christian von Mannlich showing a young woman fastening a letter to a pigeon's neck. In the First and Second World Wars the birds were used to convey messages across enemy lines, and pigeon racing remains a popular sport right up to the present day.

❈ Leopold Joseph Fitzinger, '*Ectopistes migratorius*' (Passenger Pigeon), 1864, from *Bilder-atlas zur Wissenschaftlich Populären Naturgeschichte der Vögel in ihren sämmtlichen Hauptformen.*

✻ Torii Kiyoshige, *Minamoto no Yoritomo Hiding in a Tree*, *c.* 1758, colour woodblock print.

⚹ Maker unknown, marble grave stele of a little girl, Classical Greece, *c.* 450–440 BCE, Parian marble.

⚹ René Magritte, *The Big Family*, 1963, oil on canvas.

MAGPIES

FAMILY Corvidae

A handsome bird with striking black and white plumage, most cultures consider the magpie to be clever, and in some it has a reputation as sinister, a trickster and a thief. Along with fellow corvids the raven and the crow, it has often been attributed with devilish significance in foretelling the future.

Various magpies of the genus *Pica* are found in regions of Europe, Asia and western North America, including the Eurasian (*Pica pica*), black-billed (*Pica hudsonia*) and yellow-billed (*Pica nuttallii*) species. The Oriental magpie (*Pica serica*) is found from southeastern Russia to eastern China, Korea, Japan and northern Indochina.

The Romans trained magpies, sometimes hanging their cages at the threshold of the home to greet visitors. They associated the bird with magic and fortune-telling, using it in augury, a role later reflected in William Shakespeare's *Macbeth* (Act 3, scene 4): 'Augurs, and understood relations have / By maggot pies and choughs and rooks brought forth / The secret'st man of blood'. Elsewhere its reputation was even darker. In Central Europe the magpie's white and black plumage was interpreted as a sign that it was a force of both good and evil, and in Germany it was considered a bird of the underworld. On Sweden's Walpurgis Night, which marked the start of summer, sorcerers were said to transform into magpies after riding to Blåkulla, the island or mountain where the devil held court.

A well-known legend in Christianity holds that the magpie did not enter the ark with other birds, instead preferring to sit on its roof, cackling as the world flooded; in another the bird refused to go into full mourning after the Crucifixion and was cursed as a result, unable

John Gould, '*Pica caudata*' (Magpie), 1862–73, from *The Birds of Great Britain*.

Félix Bracquemond, *Margot la Critique*, 1854, etching.

MARGOT la CRITIQUE.
Raucaque garrulitas studium que immane loquendi.

to lay an egg unless suspended from a branch nine times in succession.

The magpie has long been demonized in Britain and Ireland, the subject of much superstition and myth, and the bird appears in several English medieval manuscripts. Seeing one near the window of a house is said to foreshadow death, while the sound of a chattering magpie indicates the coming of a stranger. The popular traditional nursery rhyme 'One for Sorrow' reflects the belief that magpies can predict the future: 'One for sorrow, Two for joy, Three for a girl, Four for a boy', and so on.

The bird's distinctive chattering call has been another frequent cause of suspicion, associated with gossiping: a popular expression in French is 'to chatter like a magpie' (*bavard comme une pie*). In Scotland, magpies were said to have a drop of the devil's blood on their tongues, and that if the tongue was scratched and bled, the bird would gain the gift of human speech. The Netherlandish artist Pieter Bruegel the Elder placed a magpie on the gallows in a famous painting of 1568. While various interpretations have been made of its role in the work, one of the most popular is that the magpie represents the baseless and spiteful gossip that often leads to the gallows.

In Norway, the bird was considered cunning and thievish, and there is a widespread belief in Italian, French and British folklore that magpies have a penchant for picking up shiny metal objects and precious stones (though recent research at the University of Exeter refutes the claim's veracity). The trait forms the premise of numerous creative works, including Gioachino Rossini's opera *The Thieving Magpie*, which premiered in 1817, and the twenty-first volume of Hergé's *Adventures of Tintin*, *The Castafiore Emerald* (published 1963). The Japanese adjective *pikapika*, pronounced like the bird's scientific name, refers to the sparkle of a glittering object like a star or gemstone.

❖ Alessandro Magnasco, *The Tame Magpie* (detail), *c.* 1707–8, oil on canvas.

✻ Francisco de Goya, *Manuel Osorio Manrique de Zuñiga* (detail), 1787–88, oil on canvas.

✻

The bird enjoyed a more positive reputation beyond Europe. For many Native American peoples, the black-billed magpie was considered a friend of hunter-gatherer tribes, warning them of danger or assisting them in times of trouble. For the Cheyenne the bird is a sacred messenger of the creator deity, whereas the Hopi and other Pueblo tribes view it as a directional guardian, associated with the east. However, in some legends the magpie is again portrayed as a gossip and busybody who annoys other animals.

The first character of the Chinese word for magpie means 'happiness', and in China the bird is seen as a signifier of good fortune, with a role as the official 'bird of joy' in the Qing dynasty. In the folktale of the cowherd and the weaver girl, a bridge of magpies reunites lovers whose romance was forbidden every year on the seventh day of the seventh lunar month. Originally from a poem dating back over 2,600 years, the story remains popular in China, Japan and many other parts of Asia, with different variations adopted in different places.

In Korea, the magpie is celebrated as a bird of great good fortune and courage, a provider of prosperity and understanding, and features in many parables and foundational myths. The bird often adds a humorous element to the popular subject of the tiger, an object of awe and terror as well as of worship. The tiger was believed to expel evil spirits and the magpie to bring good news, and paintings of the pair were placed at the front gates of houses on New Year's Day to bestow good luck and fortune in the coming year.

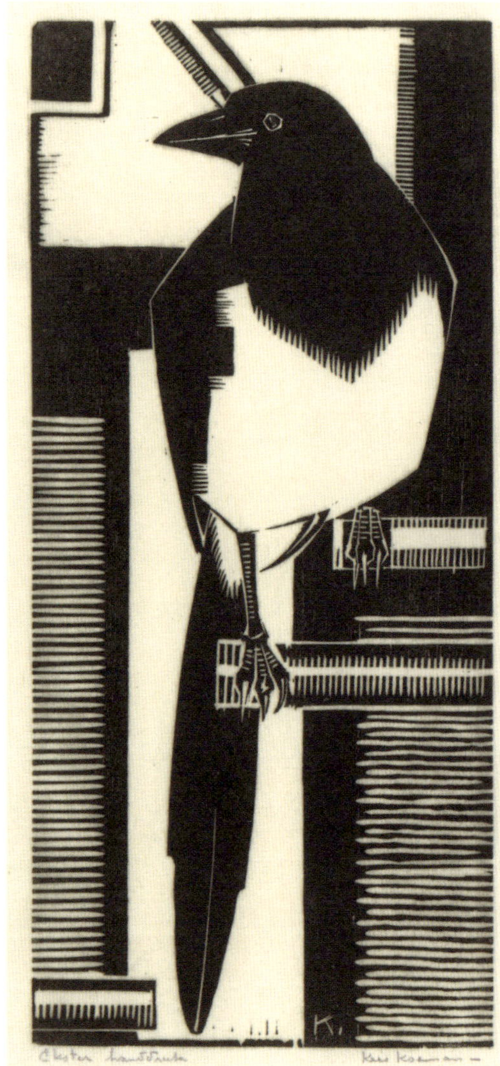

Kees Koeman, *Magpie*, 1910–32, woodcut.

Joan Miró, Plate (folio 4) from *Il était une petite pie* (Once There Was a Little Magpie), 1928, pochoir.

With large eyes, joyful song, a fearless personality and a splash of colour, the European robin (*Erithacus rubecula*) has been voted Britain's national bird several times. Its friendly disposition has historically protected it from persecution in the British Isles, though it is less highly regarded across mainland Europe and Russia.

Christian legend ties the bird to the Crucifixion, with a robin's attempt to comfort Christ on the Cross with its singing, easing his pain by pulling thorns from his head. In different versions of the narrative, either some of Christ's blood fell on the robin or a thorn pierced its breast, making it carry forever the mark of its piety. The bird is blessed by Christ, who declares it will bring happiness and joy wherever it goes. In another explanation for the flash of red, the robin's breast is scorched as it fetches water for souls stuck in Purgatory.

The identification of the robin as a comforter of the sick or dying is embedded in many northern European traditions, particularly in Britain, Ireland, France and Germany, often relating to the bird covering the dead out of respect. In the traditional sixteenth-century English tale *Babes in the Wood*, robins undertake the burial of two children, abandoned by their wicked uncle and left to die in the forest, by covering their bodies with leaves. The story's credence was enhanced by the fact that robins, as ground feeders, were often observed turning over leaves around graves when foraging for food. After the funeral of Queen Mary II in Westminster Abbey, a robin was supposed to have regularly perched on the Queen's mausoleum, leading the bird to be dubbed the 'Westminster wonder'.

Harming robins has often been linked with terrible consequences, with the English poet William Blake penning in 'Auguries of Innocence' (*c.* 1803), 'A robin redbreast in a cage / Puts all Heaven in a rage.' British and Irish superstition holds that hurting or killing a robin leads to the perpetrator's death, while breaking their eggs results in damage to valued possessions. In the Austrian Tyrol, someone who pestered a robin's nest would suffer epilepsy, while in Bohemia it was a permanent trembling of the hands. Jacob Grimm in the nineteenth century recorded a tradition in German-speaking Europe that if someone destroyed a robin's nest, their house would be struck by lightning.

Many have been moved by the robin's beautiful song, especially in the twilight hours. It offered comfort to the nineteenth-century English poet John Clare, who penned in his verse 'The Autumn Robin':

Sweet little bird in russet coat,
The livery of the closing year,
I love thy lonely plaintive note
And tiny whispering song to hear,
While on the stile or garden seat
I sit to watch the falling leaves,
The song thy little joys repeat
My loneliness relieves.

Sir Joshua Reynolds (circle of), *Babes in the Wood* (detail), *c.* 1770, oil on canvas.

John Gould, '*Erythacus rubecula*' (Robin, or Redbreast), 1862–73, from *The Birds of Great Britain.*

The English medieval manuscript the Sherborne Missal, dating from the late fourteenth or early fifteenth century, includes a remarkable portrait of a robin. Alongside the illustration is written *roddock*, the Middle English word for robin, and *Robertus*, Latin for Robert, drawing a link between the bird and the man who commissioned the manuscript, Robert Bruyning, abbot at the Abbey of St Mary in Sherborne, Dorset. The robin is also a favourite subject for Christmas cards in Britain, thought to originate from a link with Victorian postmen, who wore red jackets and were nicknamed 'redbreasts'.

A famous, somewhat macabre English nursery rhyme originating in the eighteenth century has the call and response:

Who killed Cock Robin?
I, said the sparrow,
With my bow and arrow,
I killed Cock Robin.

Various theories abound regarding who is represented by Cock Robin: possible candidates include Robin Hood, or it may relate to the death of King William II, killed in the New Forest in 1100. A fifteenth-century stained-glass window at Buckland Rectory, near Tewkesbury in Gloucestershire, depicts a robin shot with an arrow.

❖ Cesare Magni (attr.), *Madonna with Child and Robin* (detail), 1500–49, oil on panel.

✻ Walter Crane, 'Cock Robin and Jenny Wren', n.d., from *The Baby's Opera*.

COCK ROBIN AND JENNY WREN
1. 'Twas on a mer-ry time, When Jenny Wren was young, So neat-ly as she danced, And so sweet-ly as she sung, Rob-in Redbreast lost his heart, He was a gallant bird, He doffed his cap to Jenny Wren, Requesting to be heard.
2. "My dearest Jen-ny Wren, If you will but be mine, You shall dine on cher-ry pie, And drink nice currant wine; I'll dress you like a gold-finch, Or like a peacock gay, So if you'll have me, Jenny, dear, Let us appoint the day."
3. Jenny blushed behind her fan
And thus declared her mind—
"So let it be to-morrow, Rob,
"I'll take your offer kind;
"Cherry pie is very good,
"And so is currant wine;
"But I will wear my plain brown gown,
"And never dress too fine."
4. Robin Redbreast got up early,
All at the break of day,
He flew to Jenny Wren's house,
And sang a roundelay;
He sang of Robin Redbreast,
And pretty Jenny Wren,
And when he came unto the end,
He then began again.
#13,559 (nd)
Nursery Rhymes - Cock Robin & Jenny Wren 43

*

COMMON NIGHTINGALE

SPECIES Luscinia megarhynchos

The evocative, beautiful song of the common nightingale (*Luscinia megarhynchos*) – an otherwise unprepossessing, plain brown bird with a reddish tail – has captivated humans, especially poets, for centuries. The male's complex, liquid and melodious repertoire is delivered at night, meaning that it can be heard clearly, without any interference from competing birdsong.

Found in Europe and Eurasia and wintering in Sub-Saharan Africa, the nightingale was immortalized in many forms in ancient Greece. One tragic story, referenced in Homer's *Odyssey*, tells of the queen Aëdon, who accidentally kills her own son, Itys. Zeus takes pity on her and changes her into a nightingale, its song a lament for her dead son. In another myth, Philomel, daughter of the king of Athens, is raped, after which her assailant is transformed into a hoopoe and Philomel herself a nightingale, destined forever to sing a lamentation. This interpretation of the nightingale's song is repeated in Greek and Roman plays and literature, evoked by Sophocles, Aristophanes, Virgil and Ovid among others. Nevertheless, the Greeks were not averse to consuming the bird, particularly its tongue, to imbue the devourer with song.

In the twelfth and thirteenth centuries the nightingale appears in Chaucer's *Parlement of Foules* as one of many birds debating which female bird to choose for a mate, while in the Middle English poem *The Owl and the Nightingale* the two birds engage in a verbal contest with each other. The subjects they quarrel about – love, marriage, identity, cultural background, class and the right to be heard – still resonate today, with the birds taking turns to present their arguments, like in a contemporary court.

In later times the nightingale has offered a seemingly endless source of inspiration to poets, troubadours and minstrels (though most

Basil Ede, '*Luscinia megarhynchos*' (Nightingale), pl. 23, 1894, from *A Hand-Book to the Birds of Great Britain* by Richard Bowdler Sharpe, vol. I.

Max Ernst, *Two Children Are Threatened by a Nightingale*, 1924, oil on wood with painted wood elements and frame.

mistakenly attribute its song to the female rather than the male bird). John Milton's sonnet 'O Nightingale' (*c.* 1603) compares the nightingale's song to the jarring call of the cuckoo to contrast love and hate, while in his Sonnet 102 William Shakespeare draws a parallel with his own love poetry, noting that even the sound of a nightingale would become tedious if heard throughout the summer when the air is filled with other birdsong.

The nightingale's symbolism was supercharged in the Romantic poetry of the late eighteenth to mid-nineteenth centuries, with the bird held up as a marker of joy, purity, virtue and goodness; for some, it was the voice of nature itself. The most famous tributes are

by Percy Bysshe Shelley, who presents the poet as 'a nightingale who sits in darkness, and sings to cheer its own solitude with sweet sounds', and John Keats, who in 'Ode to a Nightingale' finds in the bird's song the poetry he himself so longs to write:

'Tis not through envy of thy happy lot,
But being too happy in thine happiness –
That thou, light-winged Dryad of the trees
In some melodious plot
Of beechen green, and shadows numberless,
Singest of summer in full-throated ease.

In medieval Persian literature, the nightingale often personifies a lover who is passionate and eloquent but doomed to love in vain. The object of the bird's affection is the rose, encapsulating both the perfection of earthly beauty and the arrogance inherent in such perfection. The nightingale's singing is, of course, revered for its heavenly quality too. The Persian lyric poet known by the pen name Hafez invokes the nightingale as part of a tapestry of metaphors to symbolize the deep human experience:

And each year, punctual as spring,
The new-born nightingale shall sing
Unto Musella's new-born rose;
But we shall not know anything,
Nor laugh, nor weep, not any-wise.

❖ Paul Klee, *Persische Nachtigallen* (Persian Nightingales), 1917, gouache, watercolour, and pen and black ink over graphite on laid paper, mounted on cardboard.

✻ Riza-yi 'Abbasi, *Study of a Bird*, 1634, ink, opaque watercolour, gold and silver on paper.

✻

A tiny bird with a powerful voice, the Eurasian wren (*Troglodytes troglodytes*) is a superb singer, declaring its territory throughout much of the year and brightening up a grey winter's day with a varied and hearty repertoire. Its North American counterpart, the winter wren (*Troglodytes hiemalis*), has similar plumage and is readily identified by its exuberant song.

Many legends link the wren's diminutive size to a furtive and cunning nature. In his *History of Animals*, Aristotle told a story in which all the world's birds gathered to decide which of them could fly the highest, to be crowned 'king of the birds'. The small songbirds were the first to tire, followed by the ducks, the crows and many others, until finally only the eagle remained flying, boastfully climbing ever higher. But a tiny wren had concealed itself within the eagle's feathers to hitch a ride. On revealing itself, the wren continued to fly upwards, claiming the title of king of the birds. According to the tale, the eagle was so indignant at the wren's treachery that he hurled the small bird to the ground, causing it to lose half its tail feathers.

Intriguingly, Aristotle's story finds a parallel in a Native American legend with a similar narrative, which also recognizes winter (and perhaps other) wrens as bold and resourceful birds. In all versions of this tale, the wren's

※ Bachiacca (Francesco Ubertini), *Portrait of a Woman with a Book of Music* (detail), *c.* 1540–45, oil on panel.

※ John James Audubon, '*Troglodytes hiemalis*' (The Winter Wren, 1. Male 2. Female 3. Young), no. 25, pl. 121, 1841, from *The Birds of America*, vol. II.

Charles Fréger, *Wren Boy, Dingle, Ireland*, 2014, from the 'Wilder Mann' series, photographic print.

Alex Hunt, *Kwakiutl Wren*, twentieth century, red cedar and acrylic paint.

size is a measure of its worth, symbolizing vitality, energy and cleverness. That said, a less favourable interpretation sees the wren as a cheeky and dishonest upstart, which naively believes it can fool others and win status for itself through deception.

According to some pagan traditions, the wren's short, cocked tail feathers (it is sometimes known as the cutty-tailed wren) were linked to a belief that the bird had stolen fire from the sun and brought it back down to earth. Held sacred to the earth gods and goddesses, the Druids regarded the wren as a bird of prophecy and magic, a symbol of the past year and probably connected with a midwinter celebration or sacrifice, no doubt stemming from the fact that it sings in the depths of winter. Known as 'God's bird' or 'Our Lady's hen', it was said that harm would come to any who hurt it. Along with the raven, the wren was domesticated by the Druids for its special powers, and it is one of the animals of the Celtic zodiac.

In the Middle Ages the Christian Church was keen to undermine vestiges of druidic reverence for the wren. The bird was said to have betrayed Jesus' presence in the Garden of Gethsemane, while another legend held that it had prevented St Stephen from escaping captivity by disturbing a sleeping guard, leading to his execution by stoning on 26 December. To commemorate the saint's martyrdom, on that date some communities hunted the wren with birch rods and stoned it to death. Happening on or close to the winter solstice, the ceremony supposedly marked the passage from dark powers to new light and life. People celebrated the occasion by dressing up in masks, straw suits and colourful clothing, parading the wren through towns and villages accompanied by music. In Wales, a live wren would be paraded in a decorated cage by a boy, who would sing, 'Come and make your offering, to the smallest yet the king', to which the reply came, 'Pleased to see the king'. Today, most surviving examples of wren hunting or 'wrenning' take place in parts of western Ireland, where the costuming of earlier times is retained.

The wren holds varying significance for different Native American cultures. The Pawnee call the winter wren the 'laughing bird' and a 'very happy little bird', the first to greet the rising sun with song; the Cherokee held no such regard for it though, considering it a busybody and gendering it as a 'she'. Others have identified the winter wren as an omen that affected warriors on the warpath, with the Creek viewing the bird as a 'true oracle of bad ways', especially when it sat chirping in a tree over a war camp.

A striking woodcut by the English naturalist and engraver Thomas Bewick captures the Eurasian wren's distinctive posture. John James Audubon later made his own image of the winter wren, successfully rendering its colouring, and designated the bird 'Bewick's wren' in honour of his friend. In a demonstration of the bird's popularity in Britain, from 1937 to 1960 the farthing coin featured a Eurasian wren on its reverse, chosen because it was thought to be Britain's smallest bird (a distinction that in fact belongs to the goldcrest, *Regulus regulus*).

BARN OWL

A nocturnal creature in ghostly white, with soundless flight and a fearsome call, the barn owl (*Tyto alba*) has historically been a particular target of superstition and persecution (perhaps second only to the raven), considered both wise and sinister. Yet the bird is not only harmless but positively beneficent to humankind.

Like the raven, the barn owl is found on every continent. It was a popular hieroglyphic in ancient Egypt, and an outstanding depiction is carved on a block in the 'tomb of the warriors' at Deir el-Bahari, though the 'ears' are a departure since barn owls do not possess them. A rare later sculpture of a barn owl is beautifully rendered in limestone, its heart-shaped face carved in a circle of short brown feathers, with small holes above the eyes to imitate the black-and-white speckles. Bristly feathers help to emphasize the beak.

Since ancient times owls have been held to possess wisdom and knowledge, doubtless because of their solemn demeanour and power to see in the dark. The Greek goddess of wisdom Athena was represented and accompanied by an owl (the little owl, *Athene noctua*), while in Celtic mythology the barn owl was linked to the wise old woman Crone goddess, serving as a guide through the underworld. A familiar later motif presents the owl as a learned scholar, complete with spectacles and mortarboard.

The Romans considered owls a portent of death and misfortune, especially if they called while perched on a roof. Such dark associations were absorbed into the iconography of the Christian Church, and medieval carvings and paintings depict owls (especially barn owls) accompanying monkeys, regarded as the foulest of all beasts. Hiding in darkness and afraid of the light, the bird came to symbolize Satan himself, and it was believed that witches were able to transform themselves into owls. The presence of an owl in Crucifixion scenes is considered to signify Christ's role to 'give light to them that sit in the darkness and in the shadow of death' (Luke 1:79).

British folklore is replete with superstition centred around owls. Using them to predict the weather, barn owls would be displayed in churchyards or nailed spread-eagled to barn doors to ward off lightning and evil, a practice that continued right up to the middle of the last century. Another traditional belief held that if someone walked around an owl in a tree, the bird would continue to turn its

Valentine Cameron Prinsep, *The Owl*, 1863, oil on canvas.

John James Audubon, '*Tyto alba*' (Barn Owl), no. 7, pl. 34, 1840, from *The Birds of America*, vol. 1.

head to watch them until it wrung its own neck. In parts of northern England, it was considered good luck to see an owl, but in Wales, if its flight crossed your path, it was an ominous sign. In Ireland, the bird was regarded with humour rather than fear: in Donegal, for instance, the term *screachog reilige* or barn owl (literally a 'churchyard screecher') was used to describe someone with a grating, high-pitched singing voice, especially a woman.

The bird's sinister reputation is reflected in English literature, with Chaucer writing of 'the owl which announces death' (*Parlement of Foules*) and Shakespeare that 'The Owl shriek'd at thy birth, an evil sign' (*Henry VI*, Act 5, scene 6). The Romantic poets of the eighteenth and nineteenth centuries evoked the barn owl as the favoured 'bird of doom', as in William Wordsworth's 'The Waggoner' (1805):

Yon owl! – pray God that all be well!
'Tis worse than any funeral bell;
As sure as I've the gift of sight,
We shall be meeting ghosts to-night!

In much Native American folklore, the owl's connection with death and the supernatural is profound, though the bird also represents wisdom and helpfulness and is credited with prophetic powers. The Chippewa tell stories warning children to behave or else the owl will carry them away, while in other tribes the bird is said to bring messages from beyond the grave or to deliver supernatural warnings to tribesmen who broke taboos.

Such supernatural beliefs found remarkable parallels in the folklore that was carried across the Atlantic by European settlers. *The Long Hidden Friend*, a collection of folk remedies published in the nineteenth century by Pennsylvania German printer Johann Georg Hohman, makes reference to an Amish claim that placing the heart and right foot of a barn owl on a sleeping person would compel them to answer any question truthfully, while in frontier times young German men were told to 'carry the heart of an owl in your pocket if you want to have the admiration of the girls'. In African American communities and elsewhere, the owl was intimately associated with the Grim Reaper. The barn owl's rasping shrieks and hissing noises attracted much superstition, with the bird rendered 'ghostly' by its white, humanoid face and underbelly feathers, visible in flight.

In Asia, the barn owl has both positive and negative associations, sometimes revered as a guardian spirit and at other times connected with death and considered an omen of misfortune. Lakshmi, the Hindu goddess of wealth and luck, rides a barn owl, with the flapping of its wings correlated to the flow of money. The supreme Hindu god Lord Jagannath of the holy city of Puri is sometimes given the epithet Choka Dola, 'the lord with circular eyes', drawing a parallel with the owl's round, unmoving eyes, considered a signifier of insightfulness.

Across the world, the sinister reputation of owls continues to be exploited in fiction and cinema. Their disturbing cry on a moonlit night sets the stage for trepidation and doom or adds an element of suspense and intrigue, especially in the mystery and horror genres. A more sympathetic appearance is made in the Harry Potter series of books and films, where the snowy owl Hedwig is both a much-loved pet and a magical deliverer of mail.

❖ Francisco Goya, *Witches*, c. 1797–98, oil on canvas.

✱ Maker unknown, head of a barn owl, Ptolemaic Period, 664–150 BCE, limestone and pigment.

TROPICAL & SUBTROPICAL FOREST

Described by the naturalist W. H. Hudson as perhaps 'the very loveliest thing in nature', to the many indigenous peoples of North and South America the hummingbird is a sacred creature, especially the male, which displays the widest diversity in its dazzling plumage. There are some 340 species found across the Americas, with most living in the Amazon.

The Aztecs revered these agile and feisty winged jewels as a symbol of vigour, energy and skill in warfare, honouring Huitzilopochtli, the god of sun and war, whose name means 'Hummingbird from the South'. For them the hummingbird was a sacred animal and spirit guide to the afterlife, and they believed that upon death warriors and women lost in childbirth would morph into hummingbirds and fly around heavenly gardens. Though the famed emperor Moctezuma II fell defending the capital Tenochtitlán, it is said that a green-backed hummingbird rallied his men to victory, its spirit represented by the feathers decorating his arms, legs, helmet and the corners of his cloak. The Templo Mayor at the heart of Tenochtitlán is dedicated to Huitzilopochtli along with Tlaloc, the god of rain and agriculture.

In a Maya legend the hummingbird Tzunuum was created by the Great Spirit as a very plain bird with no colour. With nothing to wear on her wedding day, the other birds took pity on Tzunuum and stitched feathers together to make her a dress. When the Great Spirit witnessed her humble and gracious response she was allowed to wear her beautifully coloured gown forever, and this was the origin of the hummingbird's unique plumage. Another story tells of the divine twins Hunahpu and Ixbalanque, who faced several trials in the underworld to overcome evil powers and even death itself.

Agostino Aglio, 'Huitzilopochtli', 1831, from *Antiquities of Mexico* by Edward King, Viscount Kingsborough.

Maker unknown, textile fragment with hummingbirds from India, *c.* 1750, linen.

Joseph Constantine Stadler, 'Large flowering sensitive plant', *c.* 1807, from *New Illustration of the Sexual System of Carolus von Linnaeus* by Robert John Thornton.

By transforming themselves into hummingbirds, they escaped from the House of Bats and lived to see the dawn. The gods were so in love with the hummingbird that they held a great celebration inviting all the other animals to honour them for their exceptional beauty and wit.

In Chilean folklore, the giant god Pillan created all the birds from his thoughts alone. On realizing that he had forgotten to make the world's tiniest bird, he took a spark from the earth's fires and breathed life into it, creating the hummingbird.

Frida Kahlo, *Self-Portrait with Thorn Necklace and Hummingbird*, 1940, oil on canvas mounted to board.

John Gould, '*Topaza pella*' (Crimson Topaz Hummingbird), 1849, from *A Monograph of the Trochilid, or Family of Humming-birds*, vol. III.

Hummingbirds of North America are deemed to be fierce fighters and protectors of their homeland and to see one is a sign of good luck for many Native American tribes, especially those of the Northwest Coast. The birds bear messages of praise and requests to Mother Earth for the Pueblos, while for the Hopi and Zuni people they help convince the gods to bring rain. In shamanic culture, the bird signifies the need to accept the painful experiences of the past and learn from them. It is also linked with infinity, as its flight pattern is in the shape of a figure 8.

A Cherokee legend says the hummingbird used his speed and swiftness to seize a piece of the world's first tobacco plant to help heal an old woman. In turn, the Navajo tell of how a plain, crow-sized hummingbird was shrunk by the Great Spirit to its present size as punishment for harming flowers. As compensation, the Great

Spirit clothed it in a palette of many colours. To many North American cultures, the bird's arrival in spring was a harbinger of moisture-bearing clouds, the magical properties of medicine and the prospect of fertility.

Not surprisingly, when colonists discovered the astonishing beauty of hummingbirds, vast numbers of their skins were used in the garment industry, for artificial flowers and in artworks. A shawl made in 1905 was composed of no fewer than 8,000 skins. In the nineteenth century, the British naturalist John Gould displayed his collection of 1,500 specimens at London Zoo and further popularized hummingbirds by producing a 360-plate monograph about them.

CASSOWARIES

Cassowaries are flightless birds native to the tropical forests of New Guinea and northeastern Australia. Outside the breeding season, they are solitary, timid and hard to spot in their natural habitat. They play a part in the spiritual narratives of many indigenous peoples of the region, often in tales of transformation.

The southern cassowary (*Casuarius casuarius*) is the world's third tallest and second heaviest living bird, with a vivid blue face, two red wattles hanging from its neck and a hollow 'helmet' known as a casque atop its head. Though appearing docile, its muscular legs pack a powerful kick, with the claw of the inner of its three claw-tipped toes reaching lengths of 12 cm (5 in.). Two smaller species inhabit New Guinea: the northern cassowary (*Casuarius unappendiculatus*) of the lowlands and the dwarf cassowary (*Casuarius bennetti*) occupying higher elevations.

Fossilized eggshells found in rock shelters in New Guinea suggest that ancient indigenous people preferred to harvest cassowary eggs rather than adult birds. They appear to have regulated their consumption, possibly even rearing young birds from the eggs as one of the earliest forms of domestication, thousands of years before the chicken. To this day societies in the New Guinea Highlands capture cassowary

'*Casuarius unappendiculatus*' (One-wattled Cassowary), 1900, from *A Monograph of the Genus Casuarius* by Walter Rothschild.

Francis Barlow, *A Cassowary*, *c.* 1680–90, oil on canvas.

chicks and raise them as semi-tame poultry for food and for use as ceremonial gifts.

The Kewa people of Papua New Guinea's Southern Highlands Province tell of an old woman who was imprisoned by a man and contracted painful indigestion when he fed her the starchy root vegetable taro. She was freed by cassowaries, who took pity on her plight, clawing her captor to death and kicking the woman's stomach to relieve the pain. To thank the birds for her release, the old woman granted the birds their striking neck colours.

In another intriguing legend from Morobe Province on the northwestern coast of Papua New Guinea, the cassowary vies with the hornbill for the best forest fruit and invariably wins. In retaliation, the cunning hornbill suggests a contest in which both birds break their wings to see what aerial feats they can perform. The hornbill imitates breaking its own wings by snapping two twigs, while the cassowary breaks its real wings and remains flightless forever after.

Indigenous stories about the cassowary's transformative abilities were recorded by Europeans and Australians. One tells of a hunter, who stood astounded as five cassowaries shed their feathers and morphed into beautiful sisters. Later, when the youngest sister was bathing, the hunter collected her feathers and carried her home. They married, had a son and enjoyed a settled life, but one day she found her feathers and decided to escape, only ever to be seen again in her feathered form.

Another human–bird transformation was reported by André Dupeyrat, a French priest who spent twenty-one years among the Papuans. In his book *Savage Papua* (1954), Dupeyrat recounts receiving a visit one evening from a reputed sorcerer, who arrived and left to the

sound of thudding cassowary feet. By morning the sorcerer had mysteriously returned to his own village, covering a mountainous five-mile trek considered impossible for humans to manage in the dark.

Cassowaries – variously called Goondoye, Gunduy, Gundulu or Kutini – are integral to the Dreamtime narratives of Aboriginal groups

in Queensland, featuring in stories, dances and ceremonies. In one tale, a wicked, louse-infested man who lived by the Murray River, preying on children and eating them, was invited into the camp of a local tribe on the promise of helping to remove his lice. When he fell asleep, the tribesmen hacked off his arms, and as he escaped, he was transformed into a cassowary with stunted wings.

Over the centuries cassowaries have been exploited for their feathers, used in ceremonial headdresses, and for their claws and bones, used as tools and daggers. Bone daggers found at the village of Auwim in East Sepik Province, Papua New Guinea, are stencilled to mark significant events and rituals. Typically, they are the full length of the bird's tibiotarsus bone, often sharpened at the edge or shaped into a needlepoint as weaponry.

In Australia, cassowary numbers have been significantly depleted due to predation of eggs and chicks by pigs and dogs, loss of rainforest and killing by road vehicles, and the southern cassowary is now considered an endangered species.

❂ Jiwaka Tribe from Western Highlands at Mount Hagen Show, Papua New Guinea, headdresses made from Cassowary feathers, 2011, photographic print.

✳ Maker unknown, dagger, Papua New Guinea, n.d., cassowary bone.

❖ Maker unknown, mask (Buk, Krar or Kara), Torres Strait Islander, mid to late nineteenth century, Mabuiag Island, Australia, turtle shell, wood, cassowary feathers, fibre, resin, shell and paint.

❖

The laughing kookaburra (*Dacelo novaeguinaea*) is a terrestrial kingfisher native to Australia and New Guinea. Its name is a loanword from the Australian Aboriginal language Wiradjuri, *guuguubarra*, onomatopoeic of its loud, distinctive call resembling human laughter. The related blue-winged kookaburra (*Dacelo leachii*) of northern Australia makes a call more like a cackling scream or even maniacal barking.

In Aboriginal mythology, the kookaburra is a messenger of good news, often depicted in art and stories as a symbol of happiness and abundance. The bird is also linked to the rainbow serpent, which represents fertility and renewal. In some tribes it is believed that the kookaburra's loud call brings rain after long droughts, and in others that if it laughs in the middle of the day it is going to rain.

According to Dreamtime narratives, there was once no sun, only a moon and stars, until one day the beautiful dancing bird Brolga was so angered by Dinewan, the emu, that she grabbed a large emu egg and threw it into the sky. Landing on firewood, the egg broke, spilling its yellow yolk, which burst into flames and lit up the whole world to the astonishment of all the creatures. Seeing how beautiful the earth looked when illuminated by this blaze, a spirit in the sky decided to make a fire every morning. This was not enough, however, as those who were sleeping did not see it, so the creator god Baiame decided a noise was needed to announce the sun's arrival. Hearing the kookaburra, Goo-goor-gaga, Baiame asked him to laugh loudly every morning as the day dawned to wake everyone up. The bird agreed and has done so ever since, charging the early morning air with laughter.

Another legend viewed the kookaburra as a very contented bird who, though unable to sing himself, never became jealous of those who could. The other birds got angry when hearing the lyrebird boast that he could sing better than anyone else and gathered to prove him wrong.

François-Nicolas Martinet, '*Dacelo novaeguinaea*' (Laughing Kookaburra), pl. 663, 1765–83, from *Planches Enluminées D'histoire Naturelle* by Edme-Louis Daubenton, vol. VII.

Mick Qulliam, *Kookaburra*, 2017, acrylic on canvas.

As each one sang, the lyrebird copied their songs more sweetly, much to the amusement of the kookaburra, who burst out laughing. Thinking this was the kookaburra's song, the lyrebird tried to copy it and was forced to admit he could not do it as well.

Australians take pride in their famous bird, celebrated in the eponymous nursery rhyme written by Marion Sinclair in 1932. For many years the call of a kookaburra nicknamed Jacko was the opening theme of the Australian Broadcasting Corporation's radio stations and overseas broadcasts. The bird appears on stamps and banknotes and a coin known as the Silver Kookaburra has been minted annually since 1990. Olly the Kookaburra was one of three mascots for the 2000 Olympic Games in Sydney, while the Kookaburra company produces hockey gear, football merchandise and cricket equipment, including the red ball used in some Test matches.

Native to the rainforests of Australia, there are two species of this ground-dwelling bird, the superb lyrebird (*Menura novaehollandiae*) and Albert's lyrebird (*Menura alberti*). Both are famous for their spectacular tail feathers and near-perfect mimicry, often of noises generated by humans, and have been venerated by Aboriginal peoples for thousands of years.

The superb lyrebird's tail consists of sixteen highly modified feathers, originally thought to resemble a lyre. This misconception originated in the 1800s, when a superb lyrebird specimen was taken from Australia to the United Kingdom. A taxidermist at the British Museum mistakenly thought the tail would be displayed like a peacock's, resembling a lyre, and arranged the feathers accordingly. In fact, in an elaborate courtship ritual the male fans and throws forward the layer of white upper tail feathers to cover his back and head. John Gould – who had also never seen a live lyrebird – later painted his depiction from the British Museum specimen.

The superb lyrebird is reputed to reproduce up to twenty different bird calls accurately, as well as those of dingoes, possums and koalas, and even appears to have developed regional dialects. Its courtship songs, delivered on a display platform, involve a cascade of warbles and trills and mimicry of other species for as long as twenty minutes. It also has an astonishing ability to mimic sounds generated by humans, including chainsaws, car alarms and engines, camera shutters, crying babies, music, ringtones, even words! The females of both species are also capable of complex vocalizations and mimicry.

The lyrebird is often described in Aboriginal Dreamtime narratives as the 'peaceful broker of the bush', the only animal able to communicate

Leopold Joseph Fitzinger, '*Menura superba*' (Superb Lyrebird), 1864, from *Bilder-atlas zur Wissenschaftlich-populären Naturgeschichte der Vögel in ihren sämmtlichen Hauptformen*.

Damian Cazaly, *The Supurb Lyrebird's Song*, 2018, mural in Rochester, Victoria, Australia.

with all the others. Koori Dreaming stories, akin to fairy tales, served to impart to the youngest members of the clan the laws that governed the cultural behaviour of clan members. Dreaming stories continued under European dominance, disguised as charming legends with animals as their heroes. Koori culture is based on ownership of information rather than property and possessions, and its people believed that children learned better and more quickly when they were encouraged to work through a problem, rather than being told the answer.

Another Dreamtime story tells of a lyrebird singing at a foaming stream, who notices a bubble rising in sync with his song. Recognizing a spirit wishing to come to life, the lyrebird watches as the bubble breaks into a little green frog. The bird takes the frog under its wing and teaches the creature to sing.

The lyrebird has appeared many times on Australian postage stamps and coins and as the emblem of various institutions and musical organizations. Sadly, the bushfires of 2019–20 damaged much of its habitat, meaning a reclassification of its status from 'common' to 'threatened' may be required. Beyond this new threat are the long-term vulnerabilities to predation by cats and foxes, as well as human pressures.

Described by some Papuan tribes as 'birds of the gods', birds-of-paradise are renowned for their courtship rituals and extravagantly colourful plumage. Many of the males have long, elaborate feathers extending from the beak, wings, tail or head, with the greater bird-of-paradise (*Paradisaea apoda*) considered the most flamboyant.

The forty species are spread across the dense rainforests of eastern Indonesia, Papua New Guinea and eastern Australia. The birds hold profound ritual and symbolic meaning for indigenous Papuan peoples, featuring extensively in folklore and oral traditions, and to this day their feathers and bodies embellish headdresses and traditional ceremonial dress so prized that they are passed on through the generations.

In Papua New Guinea, legends tell of ancestral spirits appearing in the form of birds-of-paradise and of villagers being transformed into these brilliantly coloured birds on entering the forest. Other stories describe how the birds obtained their beautiful plumes by stealing them from other creatures or spirits, with their feathers said to possess wisdom or magical powers. The feathers are worn during social rituals such as weddings and funerals to invoke these symbolic qualities, and rare plumes are considered prestige items reserved for significant occasions and high-ranking tribe members. The wearers show off this extravagant costumery in displays of dancing and to project sexual allure, much like the bird.

In the mythology of Maritime Southeast Asia, there is a notion that female birds-of-paradise drop their eggs in flight, which break on the ground to reveal a fully formed young bird ready for the world. Equally incredulous is a belief that the female lays eggs on the back of her mate, with his cushion-like plumage, and incubates the clutch sitting on the male and floating through the heavens.

The first specimens of the greater bird-of-paradise ever seen in Europe were prepared skins divested of legs and wings, which arrived in 1522, with the famed German artist Hans Baldung Grien making his drawing just a few months later. The Venetian explorer Antonio Pigafetta, who sailed with Ferdinand Magellan, recorded in his journal that the indigenous people of the East Indies told him 'these birds came from a paradise on earth and were called..."birds from God"'. Consequently, in their mounted footless and wingless state, a legend arose in Europe that the birds flew

eternally up through the clouds, drinking a special cloud dew to stay alive, and did not need legs (the specific *apoda* means 'without feet'). The belief persisted with a tale that the birds flocked en masse in southern India, where they became so intoxicated with the smell of nutmeg, they did not notice ants gnawing off their legs. Given such exceptional attributes, the bird was briefly thought to be the mythical phoenix. The first coloured image, made by Giulio Clovio, appeared in the illuminated Farnese Hours (*c.* 1540). More species arrived, often more extravagantly plumed than the last, but it would be another 150 years before birds-of-paradise were seen in Europe in their complete state.

Paul Klee, *Fairy Tale*, 1929, watercolour on gessoed canvas.

Jacques Barraband, '*Paradisaea minor*' (Small Emerald Bird of Paradise, male), 1806, from *Histoire naturelle des oiseaux de paradis et des rolliers, suivie de celle des toucans et des barbus* by François La Vaillant.

Sought after for centuries as a status symbol in China and other parts of Southeast Asia, expeditions made after their first appearance in Europe soon led to a marked expansion of trade in bird-of-paradise skins and feathers, and by the early twentieth century some 50,000 birds were being traded each year. Fortunately, hunting of the birds was eventually made illegal and by 1922 a trade embargo was imposed.

Nevertheless, during the 1940s bird-of-paradise feathers continued to be exchanged across much of Asia, long used in the Shripech royal crown worn by the former kings of Nepal and as the headgear of janissary guards at the Ottoman court in Istanbul. Despite legal safeguarding and the establishment of protected areas, illegal trade has continued in Indonesia, and the birds and their feathers remain popular

Maker unknown, Rana crown from Nepal, nineteenth century, made with pearls, precious stones and birds-of-paradise feathers.

Peter Paul Rubens, *Adoration of the Magi* (detail), 1609–28, oil on canvas.

*

in China, Europe and the United States. Some species are further endangered due to habitat destruction. Papuans were allowed to continue hunting sustainably to fulfil ceremonial needs at a local level.

Scientists note a peculiarity among the most frequently hunted bird-of-paradise species that males start to mate even before growing their ornamental breeding plumage. They suggest this may be an adaptation to maintain population levels in the face of hunting pressures, probably present for hundreds of years.

The bird-of-paradise was embraced as the national symbol of Papua New Guinea during the country's transition to independence in the 1970s, used to represent its natural heritage and cultural identity. Raggi's bird-of-paradise (*Paradisaea raggiana*), with its red-brown wirelike tail, is depicted on the national flag and as the logo for the national carrier, Air Niugini.

In a fitting tribute to these remarkable birds, the southern hemisphere constellation Apus represents a bird-of-paradise.

Native to the Indian subcontinent, the peacock (*Pavo cristatus*) – also called the Indian peafowl – was introduced to the Middle East and Europe initially by the Greeks and celebrated for its beauty and as a status symbol. The male's fanlike display, with its 200 large, quivering tail feathers, has attracted wonder for millennia.

The peacock's beautiful train and hypnotic mating dance have inspired rulers and artists alike across the Indian subcontinent, with early depictions in architecture dating back to the Indus Valley Harappan civilisation of 2500–1500 BCE. The seal of the second-century Kushan emperor Kanishka was a peacock and it appears on coins from the Gupta empire (third to sixth centuries CE).

The rulers of the later Tughlaq dynasty adopted the peacock's train feather as their state symbol and incorporated it into the headgear of their soldiers, while Jain monks carried flywhisks made of peacock feathers to ward off evil. The seventeenth-century Mughal emperor Shah Jahan commissioned a solid gold Peacock Throne festooned with jewels, which cost twice as much to build as the Taj Mahal. At the top of the throne, two peacocks face each other, representing the duality of nature central to Persian mythology.

The peacock is sacred to Hindus: Kartikeya, the god of war, rides on its back and a peacock feather adorns the crown of Lord Krishna. According to legend, when Lord Indra battled Ravana, the king of Lanka, a peacock raised its tail as a protective screen to hide him. As a reward, Indra granted the bird its blue-green plumage and exotic feathered tail with 'a thousand eyes'. In Buddhist mythology, the peacock is portrayed as a symbol of compassion and watchfulness, with one of the *Jataka* tales relating that the Buddha was a golden peacock in a previous life. Carvings of peacocks shown in a welcome pose are found on Buddhist stupas at Sanchi and Bharhut dating from the first century CE.

In China, during the Tang dynasty, peacock feathers were worn regularly at official

Artist unknown, *Kakubha-Ragini, a forlorn lady walking amongst peacocks*, c. 1775–99, gouache and gold.

Enrique Simonet, *The Judgement of Paris* (detail), 1904, oil on canvas.

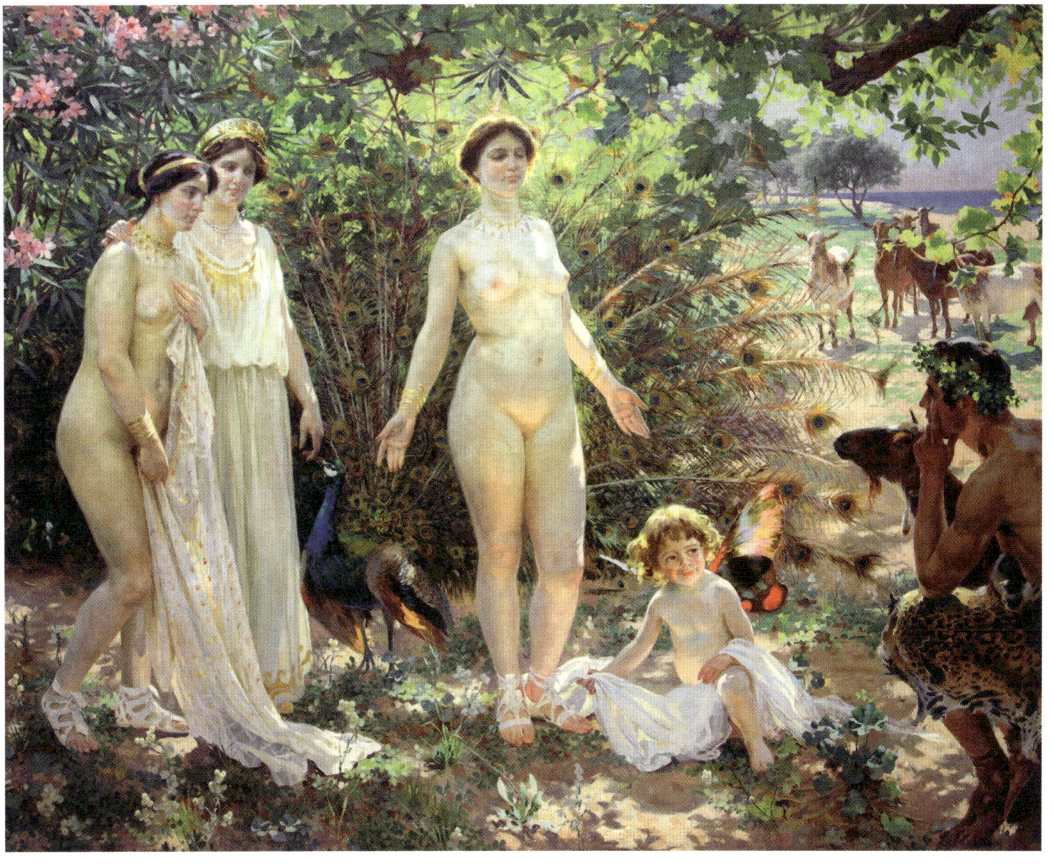

functions and paid as tributes to emperors, who awarded them in turn for faithful service, graded as 'one-eyed', 'two-eyed' or 'three-eyed' depending on the services being recognized. According to legend, a defeated Qin dynasty general sought refuge in a forest known for its peacocks. With the birds usually signalling human presence with loud screeches, this time they remained silent, so the general's enemies assumed he was not there. When he eventually became king, he honoured the peacocks by decreeing that their feathers should be awarded as a mark of bravery in battle.

Various reports relate to the peacock's introduction to the West from India. According to the Old Testament, King Solomon, who reigned around 950 BCE, received an import of peacocks from Muziris, an ancient port in Kerala. Later, during his invasion of India in 326 BCE, Alexander the Great was said to be so smitten by a flock of wild peacocks in flight that his army was warned that anyone harming these birds would be punished. In some accounts Alexander took 200 peacocks with him when he left India, the birds becoming a source of wonder in foreign lands. In Greek mythology,

❖ Joseph Smit, '*Pavo cristatus*' (Common Peafowl), 1872, from *A Monograph of the Phasianidae, or Family of the Pheasants* by Daniel Giraud Elliot.

✻ Gyorgy Kepes, *Juliet with Peacock Feather*, 1937–38, gelatin silver print with gouache.

❖

the goddess Hera had a faithful, watchful servant Argus, who had numerous eyes across his body. When Argus was killed by Hermes, herald of the gods, Hera took her servant's eyes and placed them on the peacock's tail to honour his memory.

Peacocks were introduced to Egypt in the third century BCE by the Ptolemaic rulers, where the wealthy kept them as pets and ate their meat. The Romans may have first encountered the birds displayed in cages in Ptolemy II's grand procession through Alexandria to celebrate his accession. They later bred them in large flocks for both pleasure and profit, sparking associations with vanity that endured and broadened for centuries afterwards. The peacock's impressive tail

Artist unknown (India), *Subramaniyan with his Consorts Valli and Devasena*, c. 1900–15, colour lithograph and varnish.

Alexander Calder, *Peacock*, 1941, sheet metal, wire and paint.

made the bird a natural symbol of the sky to which the dead ascend, leading to associations with immortality that were strengthened by the tail's shedding and regrowth. Some coins of Faustina the Younger, wife of Marcus Aurelius, show a peacock soaring heavenwards with the deified Roman empress on its back.

The early Christian Church borrowed this pagan emblem of immortality to use as a symbol of Christ's resurrection in funerary and ecclesiastical contexts. One of the most striking appearances in early Christian iconography is found in a fragment from an ancient mosaic floor at Aquileia in Italy, showing a peacock with its tail fanned; later, the bird was sometimes included in Renaissance paintings as a symbol of eternal life.

The peacock's associations with immortality continue to this day, with the bird used as a motif at Easter, particularly in eastern Orthodox traditions. The 'eyes' in the peacock's tail feathers are also thought to symbolize the all-seeing Christian God. Ashkenazi Jews regard a golden peacock as a symbol of joy and creativity, and it is the subject of Yiddish folktales and songs.

In many parts of medieval Europe, peacocks were kept in menageries and as garden ornaments. Heraldic peacocks were often depicted with their tails displayed, and knights took a 'vow of the peacock' to reaffirm their devotion to chivalry, decorating their helmets with the bird's plumes. But by the sixteenth century in England, peacock feathers were thought to bring misfortune, possibly associated with the 'evil eye', and a woman who wore them was committing the sin of pride.

The resplendent quetzal (*Pharomachrus mocinno*), so deserving of its name, is a small bird with shimmering metallic blue, green and red plumage that lives in upland forests of Central America and southern Mexico. During the breeding season, males develop a crest of bristly golden-green feathers and grow elongated upper tail feathers, forming a metre-long (over 3 ft) flowing train.

Much ancient folklore is centred around this almost mythical-seeming bird. It was considered divine by pre-Columbian Mesoamerican civilizations, closely associated with the Aztec god Quetzalcoatl and the Maya god Kukulkan, feathered serpents and deities of light and knowledge. To both cultures, the quetzal's green tail feathers symbolized plant growth in spring, and the bird was viewed as the 'god of the air'. Its feathers were often traded over great distances and worn by priests and royalty on ceremonial occasions.

The quetzal was thought to be the spirit guide of the Maya prince and warrior Tecun Uman, who fought the Spanish. According to legend, he was killed by the conquistador Pedro de Alvarado, and as he lay dying, a quetzal flew down and landed on his chest, dipping its feathers in the prince's blood, which is supposedly how the bird acquired its red breast and belly feathers. Another Maya tale states that the quetzal was once known for its beautiful song, but after the Spanish conquest it vowed to only sing again when the land was finally free.

Diego Muñoz Camargo, 'Battle of Michoacan between the Spanish and the Aztecs', 1892 replica of the sixteenth-century original, illustration from *Lienzo de Tlaxcala*.

John Gould, '*Trogon resplendens*' (Resplendent Trogon), 1835, from *A Monograph of the Trogonodiae, or Family of Trogons*.

Owing to the value of its feathers and the fact that it does not survive in captivity, the Maya regarded the quetzal as a symbol of wealth and freedom. The killing of quetzals was forbidden under both Maya and Aztec law, so the bird was captured to remove its tail feathers before being set free again. The Maya held the feathers so precious that they were even used as a means of exchange (to this day, the currency of Guatemala is called the quetzal). In some Mesoamerican languages, the word *quetzal* can mean 'precious' or 'sacred'.

An elaborate *quetzalcopilli* headdress now in the Museum of Ethnology, Vienna, incorporates 450 untrimmed quetzal plumes with gold appliqué, along with feathers from the cotinga, roseate spoonbill and squirrel cuckoo, all mounted on a net of vegetal fibres and wooden sticks. The headdress is thought to be 500 years old, and legend links it to the Aztec ruler Moctezuma II, who encountered the Spanish conquistador Hernán Cortés in 1519. The front is decorated with gold ornaments, and in its original state it carried a gold bird's beak.

Feather-working and the trade in feathers were underway long before the Aztec empire. They are among the precious goods held in the backpack of the old man merchant god, as depicted on the murals of the Red Temple at Cacaxtla, Tlaxcala state, Mexico (*c.* 800 CE). Elaborate feather headdresses, costumes and accessories are represented in many Maya stone sculptures and in mural paintings like those at Bonampak at Chiapas, Mexico (*c.* 792 CE), with depictions of princes preparing for the 'quetzal dance', donning heavy backpacks with the aid of attendants and long quetzal feathers. Research on the Bonampak paintings has revealed that Maya artists used a double-layered technique of blue on green against a red base, an innovation

that allowed a more accurate representation of the feathers' shimmering quality to convey divine significance. After the Spanish conquest, feather-workers transformed their practices to represent new subjects, making 'feather paintings' of devotional Christian images.

Having been embedded in the region's myths and legends for over 2,000 years, the resplendent quetzal was declared Guatemala's national bird in 1871. It is pictured on its flag and coat of arms, as well as on stamps, currency and countless souvenirs, while artistic, humanitarian and scientific endeavours are awarded by the Order of the Quetzal as the country's highest honour. Clearly, the bird's enormous cultural significance endures.

❈ Maker unknown, quetzal feather headdress, sixteenth century, quetzal feathers, gold appliqué and fibre net.

✻ Reproduction of the eighth-century Bonampak Murals, Room 1, from the Mayan temple, Bonampak, Lacandon jungle, Chiapas.

❈

*

PARROTS

Often kept as pets for their amusing, intelligent and affectionate nature, several of the 359 species of parrot are astonishingly imitative of many sounds, including human speech. On all continents, these gaudy and raucous birds have served as symbols of wealth and royalty, their feathers used for decoration and ceremony.

The indigenous peoples of South America have maintained an intimate relationship with parrots for at least 10,000 years, with shamans attaching feathers of the scarlet (*Ara macao*) and blue-and-yellow (*Ara ararauna*) macaws to their rattles to contact higher powers. The Moche people of ancient Peru worshipped parrots, considering them sacred and often depicting them in their art.

The Bororo tribe in Brazil wear astonishing crowns and bodily ornaments with macaw tail feathers, prized for their cultural significance, with various types and colours worn by different clans. In northeastern Bolivia, those performing the Macheteros dance in the Beni region sport macaw headdresses shaped like the dawning sun, reflected in the coat of arms of Beni's capital, Trinidad.

In the ancient Chinese Shang dynasty, jade artefacts were crafted in the shape of parrots to be burned along with livestock and other jade objects as part of ritual sacrifices to the gods and ancestors. The bird often appears in Chinese Buddhist iconography and scripture. One story tells of a parrot carrying water to try to put out a forest fire, which so moved the ruler of heaven that he sent rains to extinguish the flames. Another tells of how Amitābha, the principal Buddha in Pure Land Buddhism, once changed himself into a parrot to help convert people.

Leopold Joseph Fitzinger, '*Ara macao*' (Scarlet Macaw), 1864, from *Bilder-atlas zur Wissenschaftlich-populären Naturgeschichte der Vögel in ihren sämmtlichen Hauptformen.*

Peter Paul Rubens, *Holy Family with a Parrot*, 1613–15, oil on panel.

In some depictions, a parrot swoops gracefully holding a pearl or prayer beads in its beak, its gaze fixed on the deity Guanyin, who in turn welcomes the bird with a willow branch and a vase of pure water or divine nectar.

In Hindu mythology, the parrot is the mount of Kamadeva, the god of love and desire, and the parrot vahana or vehicle is sometimes painted on the bride's feet in traditional Hindu marriage ceremonies. It is also associated with the goddess Meenakshi, who is often pictured with a green parrot on her right hand, and Andal, the only female among the twelve Hindu poet-saints of India.

The people of the Marquesas Islands in Polynesia tell of a hero undertaking a long and dangerous voyage to the legendary island of Aotona (thought to be the Cook Islands)

to obtain the highly prized feathers of a red parrot as gifts for his son and daughter. Most of his rowers died of hunger on the voyage, but the survivors reached Aotona and captured enough parrots to fill 140 bags with their feathers.

Aristotle thought parrots reaching Greece from the east were allowed wine, as they were becoming 'more saucy than ever'. Alexander the Great brought some back from India, and the Alexandrine parakeet (*Psittacula eupatria*) was named in his honour. Rose-ringed parakeets (*Psittacula krameri*) from India and African greys (*Psittacus erithacus*) were trained by the Romans to perform tricks; a painting found at Herculaneum depicts a harnessed parakeet pulling a tiny chariot holding a grasshopper. The emperor Elagabalus fed parrots to his lions and the birds' heads to his staff.

Their appearance in bestiaries and manuscripts indicates that parrots were familiar in medieval England, though only the rose-ringed was known. Henry VIII owned an African grey and James V of Scotland had similar pets. Many more species were discovered in South America in colonial times, when the Catholic Church deemed the parrot's cleanliness next to God and untouched by sin; several popes prized parrots. The birds began to be included in religious paintings, to add an air of exoticism to scenes of the Garden of Eden, for instance; in Peter Paul Rubens's *Holy Family with a Parrot* (1613–15), it could perhaps symbolize the Church or the Holy Spirit. In the late Middle Ages, the Virgin Mary was sometimes depicted with a parrot, an association that led to the name Polly (a diminutive of Mary) being used for the bird.

As well as their beauty, parrots have been prized principally for their astonishing powers of mimicry, especially of the human voice, which boosted their popularity as pets. The ancient Chinese *Book of Rites* notes that the parrot can speak yet is nothing more than a bird, while in Aesop's fable of the Parrot and the Cat, the noisy bird presents a contrast with the quiet feline, with both having to learn how to coexist in the household amicably. Edouard Manet's painting of a woman with a parrot (1866) suggests a strong bond between pet and owner, perhaps even evoking the sexual connotations of the bird that date back to Classical times. Unsurprisingly, the capture of parrots as pets and for display, especially in South America, led to their scarcity, with many species threatened with extinction and some eradicated.

❖ Frida Kahlo, *Me and My Parrots*, 1941, oil on canvas.

✳ Artist unknown (China), *Guanyin, Bodhisattva of Compassion*, eighteenth century, gold ink on indigo dyed paper, mounted as a hanging scroll.

✳

The Neotropical toucans, of which there are forty species, often possess very large and colourful beaks, some four times the size of their heads and almost as long as their bodies. Symbolic of playfulness and intelligence, the birds are thought magical by many indigenous people but have been subject to much ridicule in the West.

Various explanations have been offered for the 'excess' of a toucan's beak: the extreme length helps the bird to reach fruit at the end of delicate branches; they serve as a cooling device, enhance courtship display, and help to ward off potential predators and rivals. The birds were (and still are) hunted for food and kept as pets. The beaks were a source of medicine for native populations, and a breathtaking mix of dark and brightly coloured feathers were used as body ornamentation.

One elaborate display worn by the Jivaro people of eastern Peru includes nineteen upper mandibles and eight near-intact skins. Another impressive Jivaro ornament, worn on the back, comprised oilbird bones and toucan and cotinga feathers, adorned with the wing cases of iridescent beetles. So tempting was the

Raymond Monvoisin, *Dom Pedro II, Emperor of Brazil, at age 21* (detail), 1847, oil on canvas.

John Gould, '*Ramphastos vitellinus*' (Channel-billed Toucan), 1852, from *A Monograph of the Ramphastidae, or Family of Toucans.*

exceptional colour of toucan feathers that the nineteenth-century Brazilian emperors Pedro I and Pedro II wore a ceremonial cape made from the yellow breasts of channel-billed toucans (*Ramphastos vitellinus*).

In some parts of Central and South America, the bird is associated with evil spirits and thought to be the incarnation of a demon. In Ecuador, a toucan (perhaps the red-billed toucan, *Ramphastos tucanus*) was believed to be an arrow-bearing sorcerer and to carry disease. Certain tribal religions decreed that a new father had to forgo toucan flesh as it might bewitch the newborn child and cause them to die. Toucans also served as tribal totems, considered sacred birds and messengers between the spirit world and the realm of the living, and were used by medicine men to fly to the spirit world and to cure victims of witchcraft. According to one Aztec myth, the toucan's beak was formed from a rainbow, and the bird was worshipped in the hope of the gods sending rain.

Toucans have been objects of ridicule as well as of worship. A Brazilian legend tells of how the other birds accepted the toucan as their king when it was hidden inside a hole in a tree, with only the size of its bill visible, but when it revealed itself, the other birds mocked it for being 'nothing but nose'. The word used for the toco toucan (*Ramphastos toco*, the largest in the family) by the indigenous Ayoreo people of the Gran Chaco region in Paraguay, *carai*, is also the name for a honey hunter, both presumably possessing the ability to successfully locate a food source.

When Westerners first encountered toucans in native villages of the Amazon in the sixteenth and seventeenth centuries, they found them held captive for their meat and as pets. It was not long until the birds were added to private collections in the West, making the occasional appearance in public zoos. Toucans were popularized by the English ornithologist John Gould, who published two editions of a detailed monograph on the family in the 1830s, and subsequent artists rendered them in full glory for a fascinated public. Unusually for the time, artist and illustrator Edward Lear drew from life wherever possible and even sketched inside the aviary of London Zoo in Regent's Park.

Maintaining the bird's image as a figure of fun, an advertising campaign for Guinness stout in the 1930s and 40s featured the toco toucan, its black and white colouring reflecting that of the beer.

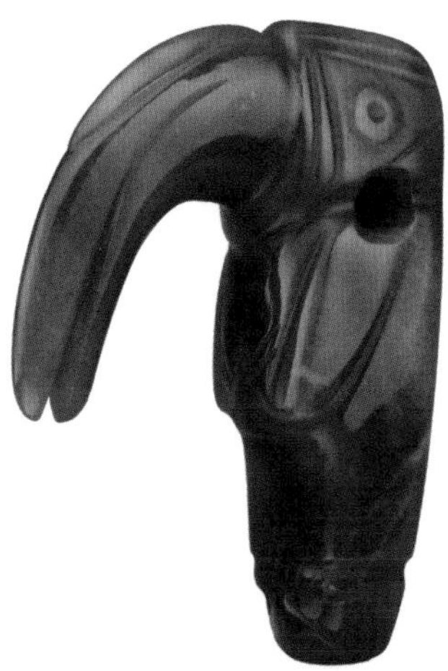

❖ Maker unknown, bird pendant from Costa Rica, 300–700 CE, jadeite.

✻ 'Guinness is Good For You', design by John Gilroy, 1928, modern pub sign, Kilarney, Ireland.

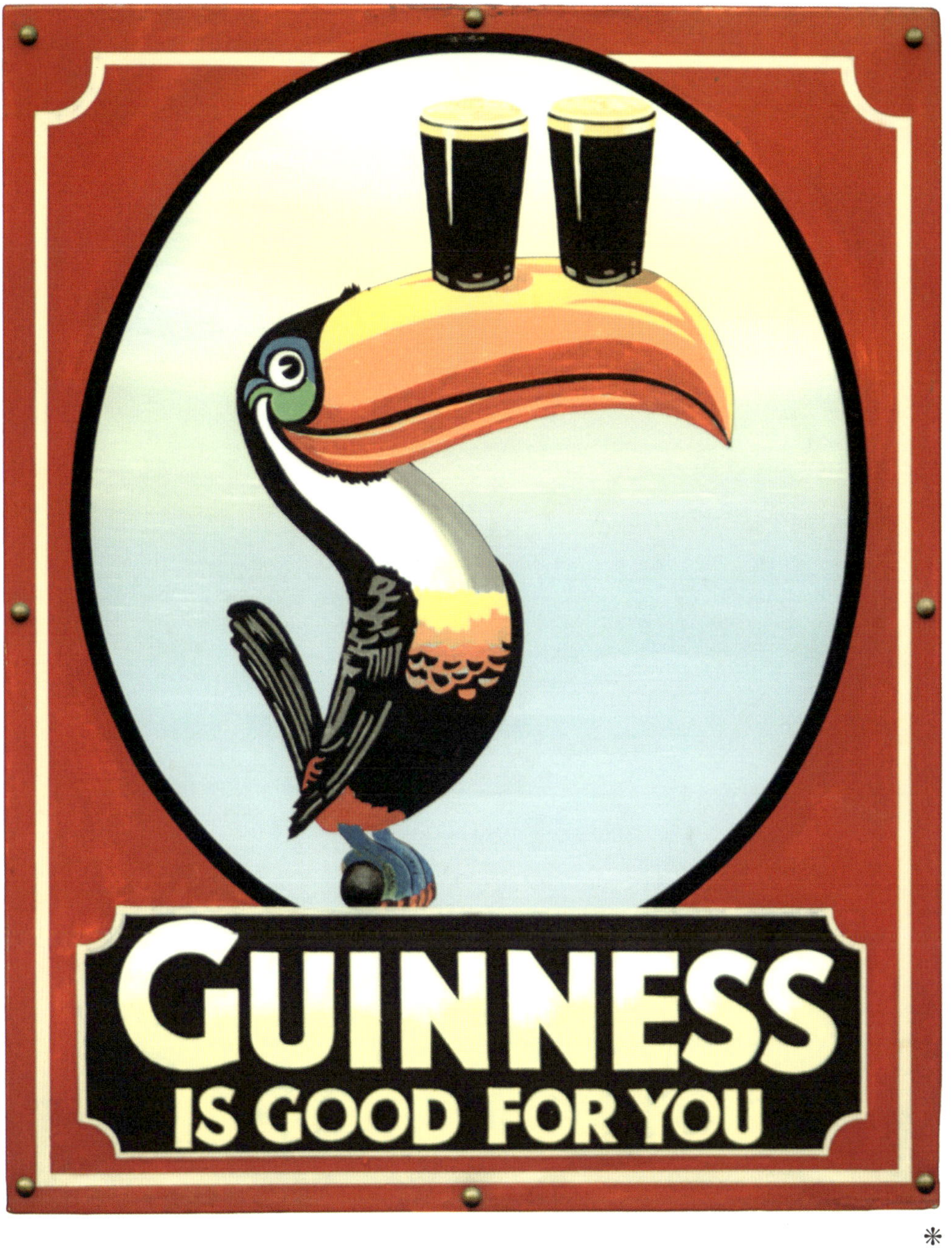
GUINNESS
IS GOOD FOR YOU

MOUNTAINS

From the earliest recorded history, cultures across the northern hemisphere have revered the golden eagle (*Aquila chrysaetos*) as the 'king of the birds'. With its ability to fly towards the midday sun, soaring until lost to sight, many have adopted it as the symbol of their most powerful gods and institutions.

The ancient Mesopotamian thunderbolt god Anzu appears as a lion-headed eagle and the bird was regarded as an omen, foretelling the unseen, while in Egypt inscriptions of eagles on the temple walls at Luxor reflect the devotion accorded the bird.

In Greek mythology, the king of the gods Zeus took the form of an eagle to abduct the young Trojan prince Ganymede, with whom he had fallen in love, a scene later made popular by old master painters including Peter Paul Rubens. Zeus' Roman equivalent, Jupiter or Jove, was also represented by the bird and honoured with a constellation in the night sky: Aquila, meaning eagle in Latin. When a dead Roman emperor was deified (known as an 'apotheosis'), an eagle was freed over the funeral pyre to convey his soul to the heavens.

Pliny calls the eagle the 'most honourable and strongest of birds' and describes it fighting a gigantic snake that wraps itself so tightly around the bird that the two appear as a two-headed animal. The image resonates as a symbol of the battle between good and evil, later summoned by Percy Bysshe Shelley in his poem 'The Revolt of Islam' (1818): 'The Snake and Eagle meet – the world's foundations tremble!'

The Roman army adopted the eagle standard as the collective emblem of an entire legion, the bird standing with outspread wings upon a thunderbolt, surmounted on a pole. When the legion was stationed in a camp, the standard was lodged in a special chapel and received veneration as the company's own divine protector. The loss of an eagle standard in battle brought great dishonour to the legionnaires.

The eagle was associated with Odin, the Norse god of war and death and of wisdom and poetry. Its cry signified the birth of a heroic soul sitting atop Yggdrasil, the great ash tree that joins up the whole universe.

In Christian mythology, the golden eagle became a symbol of resurrection and even of Christ himself, founded on a belief that the bird

※ John Gould, '*Aquila Chrysaetos*' (Golden Eagle), 1862, from *The Birds of Great Britain*, vol. I.

※ Damiano Mazza, *The Rape of Ganymede*, c. 1570–90, oil on canvas.

renewed its youthful plumage and vigour by periodically flying towards the sun and then plunging aflame into water. The identifying attribute of St John the Evangelist was an eagle, the visionary saint characterized by the winged animal who most closely reaches the heavens. A portrait of St John in the Lindisfarne Gospels (720 CE) shows an eagle carrying a bible. The bird's plumage is very well illustrated for the time, showing each feather's central shaft and two rows of barbs, and the beak realistically drawn, suggesting the illumination was created with a bird at hand. An eagle delicately crafted in wood or brass can often be seen on church lecterns to this day, supporting the bible, its outstretched wings symbolizing the spread of Christianity.

The parental care shown by the eagle towards its offspring was thought to have earned the bird God's protection. Yet less positive associations emerged too. The observation that stronger nestlings often killed the weaker ones – in a phenomenon known as 'Cainism', from the biblical tale of Cain, who murdered his younger brother Abel – gave the bird a reputation for stealing infants from cribs and killing domestic animals. A popular medieval myth, depicted in a twelfth-century bestiary, held that female eagles coerced their young to look directly into the sun, and that failure to do so without their eyes watering led to the eaglet being cast out of the nest.

Nevertheless, the bird was often held to have curative powers. Like the raven and the swallow, the eagle was believed to keep a magic stone in its nest to help when laying its eggs, and these stones were hunted to assist in childbirth. Such associations extended to the use of the bird's body parts for healing purposes throughout the British Isles, especially in the Middle Ages.

The eagles of Snowdonia (in Welsh *eryri*, 'the places of eagles') in North Wales were thought to possess mysterious powers: a golden eagle flying high foretold the birth of a great hero or victory in battle, while one flying low over valleys and uttering a cry predicted death

❈ Maker unknown, Roman eagle statue, 100–200 CE, bronze.

✱ Artist unknown, eagle-headed supernatural being from Nimrud, Neo-Assyrian Period, ninth century BCE, gypseous alabaster relief.

or disease. A lone eagle in the mountains was seen as a portent of the imminent arrival of an enemy, while a pair was a symbol of peace. In the Welsh folkloric tales of the *Mabinogion*, the warrior and magician Lleu Llaw Gyffes escapes death from a hunter's spear by assuming the shape of an eagle. Eventually, the magician Gwydion restores him to human form.

The golden eagle is paramount in the mythology and way of life of hunting peoples in Central and Northeast Asia. In pre-Islamic belief it was viewed as the host of the skies and the rains, equal in status to Allah himself, with the word for the species allied to 'father' and even 'God'. Natives of Siberia believed that the first shaman was born of an eagle or learned his arts from one. They viewed the bird as the creator of light and its children as spirit birds sitting on the branches of the world tree, topped by the double-headed eagle that is today the state symbol of Russia, seen on its coat of arms. The benevolence accorded eagles in Central Asia is like that held by Native Americans, yet quite unlike many other cultures, and it is tempting to muse that such associations were carried across the Bering Strait from Asia.

Evoking parallels with Middle Eastern and European myths, several Native American cultures represent the eagle as a 'thunderbird', a mythical super bird, identified with both the golden eagle and the bald eagle (*Haliaeetus leucocephalus*), that created thunder and lightning by beating its wings. An emblem of power, the symbol sits regally atop totem poles throughout the Pacific Northwest. As the supreme chief of natural spirit energies, the golden eagle is said to dwell in regal solitude in mystic cedar forests where no human is allowed.

It was undoubtedly the Plains tribes who made the most striking use of feathers in their iconic war headdresses, made with the white tail feathers of 'black' (immature) eagles, with those of the golden eagle the most coveted. Upwards of sixty feathers were drawn from as many as five birds and underpinned with plumes plucked from the underside of the tail. In some tribes, the earning of a feather was required to marry, have children, or partake in tribal councils.

The Plains Indians' Sun Dance ceremony of sacrifice and thanksgiving used eagle feathers to help deliver the dancers' prayers to the Great Spirit. During the Sioux Eagle Dance, participants wore eagle costumes and mimicked the bird's movements, frequently blowing eagle-bone whistles and flutes. Should a feather be dropped during a Creek or Cherokee Eagle Dance, the ceremony was stopped and a special cleansing ritual performed. For the Tewa, the Eagle Dance itself may be part of a curing rite, and the chief of the Zuni Eagle people brushed the sick with eagle feathers.

The symbolic power invested in the golden eagle remains strong worldwide to this day, and it stands as the most common national animal, representing the might of the state and other political entities. In its use as iconography on official flags and seals, it is second only to the sun, moon and stars.

Photographer unknown, Totem poles of the Haida (left) and Kwakwaka'wakw (centre) at Thunderbird Park in Victoria, British Columbia, Canada, 1955, photographic print.

Robert Rauschenberg, *Canyon*, 1959, oil, pencil, paper, metal, photograph, fabric, wood, canvas, buttons, mirror, taxidermied eagle, cardboard, pillow, paint tube and other materials.

Edward S. Curtis, *The Eagle Catcher*, 1908, photographic print.

GOLDEN EAGLE *Aquila chrysaetos*

With its intelligence, sepulchral voice, funereal plumage and heavy pickaxe beak, the common raven (*Corvus corax*) has historically been perceived as ominous on both sides of the Atlantic. Yet the bird has also been imbued with human attributes and revered as a spiritual figure or deity, especially on either side of the Bering Strait.

According to Greek legend, the god Apollo turned the raven black after the bird told him that his mistress had wed. The Romans held it to be the chief bird of omen and soothsayers attempted to foretell future events by the bird's colour, behaviour and flight. The raven's raucous cry was believed to say 'cras cras', in Latin 'tomorrow, tomorrow', encouraging faith in better times.

The raven was the first creature to be released from the ark, with Noah telling it to determine the depth of the floodwaters. When the bird failed to return, 'Noah cursed it, saying, May God make thee contemptible among men, and let carrion be thy food' (Genesis 8:7). Next Noah released a dove, which returned to the ark carrying an olive branch, proof that the flood was retreating. The contrasting behaviour of the two birds was construed as representing the two natures of man, with the raven as the base, earthly body and the dove the spirit.

In the Qur'an, it is the raven who instructs Adam and Eve how to bury their son Abel after he was murdered by his brother Cain, while the Old Testament notes the bird's fondness for isolated places (Isaiah 34:11). A warning in the

John James Audubon, '*Corvus corax*' (Raven, Old Male (Thick-Shell bark Hickory)), no. 45, pl. 224, 1842, from *The Birds of America*, vol. IV.

Katsushika Hokusai, *The Little Raven with the Minamoto Clan Sword*, *c.* 1823, colour woodcut.

Book of Proverbs (13:17) reflects the common knowledge that a raven investigating a hanged corpse would first pluck out the eyes.

The New Testament evokes the bird to illustrate that God will provide. In Luke 12:24, Jesus tells a parable about the raven to preach that people should rely on God and not riches for their needs, while in Kings 17:6 the bird is a kindly figure, feeding the needy in hard times. The hermit St Paul received sustenance from a raven after fleeing to the desert to escape persecution, a scene later depicted by the Italian Baroque painter Guercino (1660) and other artists.

Later, the raven's reputation as a prophet and soothsayer took on magical dimensions, including transmutation into a human form or vice versa, though as a result of its colour and appetite for spoiled flesh it also became a symbol of the devil. Some legends noted the bird's intelligence and facility to mimic human speech, endowing the bird with dark forces and taking its strength and dominance to portend success in battle. To the Druids it was a sacred bird and the Irish domesticated it to benefit from the auguries offered by its croaks. Ancient Britons evoking the supernatural were said to possess 'raven's knowledge'. In the Old English epic poem *Beowulf* (*c.* 975–1025), the bird is perceived as both bearing 'sinister associations with death and carnage' and as a 'joyous harbinger of the bright, radiant morning'.

Ravens feature prominently in Native American cultures, with roles as ambiguous as those attributed to owls. To this day, they are honoured as unearthly and invested with extraordinary knowledge and power. For many Northwest Indian tribes, the raven is revered as the creator of the earth, moon, sun and stars, a benevolent, transformative figure aiding people and shaping their world. By contrast, other tribes along the Pacific Northwest Coast regard the bird as a troublemaker. The Sioux occupying the Great Plains told of a white raven who warned a herd of buffalo about an approaching hunting party. The herd stampeded and the hunters were left hungry. In retaliation, an angry shaman threw the bird into a fire and turned it black.

In Chinese folklore, the raven is a celestial messenger of Xi Wangmu, the Queen Mother of the West. The emblem of the ancient Zhou dynasty was a red raven, and the Manchu people fed the birds in the belief that they were the spirits of their ancestors. According to legend, ravens would build burial mounds

❖ Chief Charles Edenshaw, *Raven Transformation Mask*, 1880, Haida Gwaii, British Columbia, Canada, cedar wood, feathers, fur, leather, string and nails.

✱ Paul Gauguin, *Nevermore*, 1897, oil on canvas.

*

for distinguished people, and, like the crow, to hear the croak of a raven is generally considered unlucky, but at certain times of day it can be an auspicious sign.

The raven is frequently evoked in Western art and literature as a symbol of death, danger and wisdom, and it is typical of the contradictions surrounding the bird that it was associated with the great hero King Arthur yet remained an emblem of misfortune. But characterizations of the bird have not been universally grim: sometimes it is playful and curious. In Charles Dickens's novel *Barnaby Rudge* (first published in 1841), the title character has a talking pet raven, Grip, which is based on a bird with the same name owned by the author. Most scholars agree that Edgar Allan Poe's famous poem 'The Raven', written a few years later in 1845, was inspired by Dickens's character, with the novel's description of the bird echoed in the lines:

In there stepped a stately Raven of the saintly
days of yore;
Not the least obeisance made he; not a minute
stopped or stayed he;
But, with mien of lord or lady, perched above
my chamber door –

In turn, the title of Paul Gauguin's 1897 painting *Nevermore*, in which the raven on the window ledge lends to an uneasy atmosphere, is taken from Poe's poem.

A famous legend persists that England will not fall to a foreign invader while ravens remain in the Tower of London. Though often taken to be an ancient belief, many consider the superstition a romantic Victorian invention.

Passionate, erotic, swift: the peregrine falcon (*Falco peregrinus*) has for centuries been revered and imbued with magical attributes, all honouring its intimate relationship with humans. Now popularly known as the peregrine, it is the fastest animal on earth, diving for prey at speeds of at least 390 km/h (242 mph) before it strikes.

Tales of the peregrine's extraordinary feats in flying are legion: in 1595, a peregrine identified with a metal band escaped from Henry IV of France's palace at Fontainebleau, only to be recovered the next day in Malta, having flown 2,170 km (1,350 miles).

With such mastery of the air, many cultures have heralded the bird as both a spiritual symbol and an aid in warfare. The prominent ancient Egyptian sky god Horus appeared in the form of a falcon (peregrine or lanner) whose right eye was the sun and left eye the moon, and the bird became associated with the Greek sorceress Circe in Classical times. In Ovid's *Metamorphoses*, the great warrior Daedalion, grief-stricken over the death of his daughter Chione, casts himself off Mount Parnassus, but the god Apollo takes pity on him, transforming him into a falcon before he hits the ground. Daedalion's courage and rage at his daughter's death endowed the bird with its exceptional strength. In Norse mythology, the god Odin was sometimes depicted with a pair of falcons, which he used to spy on the world.

For Native Americans of the Mississippian culture (*c.* 800–1600), the peregrine was a bird-man deity moving between the upper and middle worlds, serving as a messenger of the gods. Its tail feathers were worn only by shamans and helped to transform a human figure into the embodiment of a falcon, often called a 'falcon warrior'. The image – embossed in copper, engraved on shells, modelled in clay and sculpted in stone – has been found in earthwork mounds excavated during the last century. The Mississippians used dance, gestures and sounds as symbolic powers, wearing ceremonial clothes and carrying sacred objects and weapons to align themselves with the spirit world and gain favour to win victory in battles or competitions. The Creek, Choctaw, Cherokee, Seminole and Chickasaw nations retain some elements of the Mississippi culture, including sacred rites, myths and symbols such as the thunderbird.

The peregrine has been used in falconry for more than 3,000 years, first by nomads in Mesopotamia and Central Asia. Europeans praised the bird's agility and love of hunting while maintaining a calm disposition: climbing effortlessly and circling above the falconer to wait for game to be flushed out before executing a swooping dive at high speeds to strike its quarry. After the gyrfalcon (*Falco rusticolus*), the peregrine was the favoured bird in European falconry, first mentioned in England in the eighth century during the reign of King Ethelbert II of East Anglia. The sport gained favour after the Norman Conquest, remaining popular throughout the medieval period and well into Tudor and Stuart times. To train them at an early age, young wild birds were captured, especially in North Wales and Scotland.

Allegorical links between hunting, falconry and passionate courtship were first proposed and skilfully developed in the twelfth century by the French courtier Andreas Capellanus in his treatise of courtly love *De Amore*. For him, falconry was the practice that best mirrored the strategies employed by gentlemen of the middle classes who incorrectly pursued noble ladies. The association continued in medieval England, where lords and ladies borrowed metaphors from falconry to describe romantic

Mirza 'Ali (attr.), *Princely Hawking Party*, *c.* 1570, ink, opaque watercolour and gold on paper.

John Gould, '*Falco peregrinus*' (Peregrine Falcon), 1862–73, from *The Birds of Great Britain*.

relationships: expressions such as 'wrapped around the little finger' and 'feeding from the glove' derive from the sport.

An image in the German medieval illuminated manuscript the Codex Manesse shows a woman embracing a man who holds a falcon nibbling on a snack. The implication is that, while she is in the 'dominant' position now, he is nevertheless in control of both the falcon and the relationship: the woman will bend to his will and 'eat out of his hand'. Such messages find reflection in the frequent references to falconry made in Shakespeare's plays, for instance in *The Taming of the Shrew* (Act 4, scene 1), where Petruchio evokes the methods for taming falcons as a metaphor for those needed to subjugate his strong-willed wife.

In 'The Squire's Tale' from Chaucer's *Canterbury Tales*, the heroine Canace intervenes on discovering a wounded bird in a tree:

A falcon peregrine she was, and she
Seemed from a foreign land; and as she stood
She fainted now and then for loss of blood,
Till almost she had fallen from the tree.

Learning that the peregrine has been abandoned by her lover, a tercelet, Canace offers sympathy. The narrative explores how the relationships of birds mirror those of humans in subtle but unmistakable ways.

With the rise of firearms for hunting, falconry peaked in the seventeenth century before fading in the late eighteenth and nineteenth centuries. In Britain it enjoyed a resurgence in the late nineteenth and early twentieth centuries, driven largely by the pursuit of game, especially over moorlands.

Maker unknown, incised whelk shell cup showing falcon-warrior from Spiro, Oklahoma, *c.* 1100, marine shell.

Maker unknown, inlay of the Horus falcon on the hieroglyph for 'gold', Late Period–Ptolemaic Period, fourth century BCE, faience.

Maker unknown, *Hawking Party* (detail), *c.* 1500–30, wool warp and wool wefts.

In the North American colonies, however, hunting with birds gave way to guns trained on falcons and other birds of prey when they threatened domestic fowl and game birds. There is no evidence of any falconry by native peoples, while Spanish conquistadors in Mexico only briefly practised the sport, and even an early New England pilgrim falconer showed little interest.

John James Audubon called the peregrine the great-footed hawk and painted two 'Pirates' eating their 'déjeuner à la fourchette' (breakfast with a fork); he humorously noted that they were 'congratulating each other on the savouriness of the food in their grasp [gadwall and green-winged teal], but they are in fact gluttons'.

ANDEAN CONDOR

SPECIES Vultur gryphus

Carried by currents of warm air, the Andean condor (*Vultur gryphus*) circles endlessly across the highest ranges of the Andes mountains. The largest raptor in the world, boasting a wingspan of 3 metres (10 ft), it has been revered in the region for millennia, considered divine and a messenger of the gods.

The condor has been represented widely in Andean art, ceramics and textiles since about 2500 BCE, and plays an integral part in the region's indigenous religions. In a powerful symbolic triumvirate shared and worshipped by many local cultures, the condor (representing the heavens) was linked with the puma (the middle world, or earth) and the snake (the underworld). It was associated with the sun deity and ruler of the upper world, and the Inca believed that every morning it was the condor who moved the sun into the sky.

Since prehistoric times, there was widespread hunting and killing of condors for their bones and organs, which were thought to have medicinal value. At the archaeological site of Chavín de Huántar in middle Peru, a 3,000-year-old corridor has been uncovered, dubbed the 'condor's passageway' after the discovery of a large ceramic piece decorated with what appears to be the head and wings of a condor. It is likely that the corridor leads to other chambers in what was once a massive temple complex of the ancient Chavín culture.

One of the geoglyphs found in the soil of the Nazca Desert in southern Peru, created between 100 BCE and 800 CE, is in the form of a condor. At 134 metres (440 ft) long, it is among the largest of the more than 700 such works in the desert, perhaps created for the gods to gaze down on, as an astronomical calendar to help in planting and harvesting, or as pathways for important ceremonial processions. The condor also appears on textiles and painted ceramics made by the Nazca people, thought to be associated with the ritual collection of 'trophy heads'.

Thanks to its eating habits as a scavenger, the condor has a strong connection with predation, death and sacrifice. It was highly significant to the Moche people who lived along the arid coast of northern Peru around 100–750 CE, often embellishing knives used for ritual sacrifice or shown pecking at the heads and body parts

of humans and animals. Ear flares, crafted by Moche metalworkers and adorned with condors with massive talons and strong, curved beaks, may have been worn by an individual performing a sacrifice. Elsewhere, those living in the hinterland of the city of Tiwanaku, which stood on the shores of Lake Titicaca, Bolivia, from around 590 to 1150 CE, frequently observed condors scavenging the corpses of humans and other animals and incorporated naturalistic depictions of the fearsome bird into their rituals.

The Inca people believed the condor to transport the spirits of the dead, conveying them from the earthly realm to the celestial sphere. At the citadel of Machu Picchu in Peru, dating from around the thirteenth to sixteenth centuries, a natural rock formation was skilfully shaped into the outspread wings of a condor in flight to create the Temple of the Condor. To complete the figure of a three-dimensional

Maker unknown, earflare with condor, sixth or seventh century, Peru, Moche, silver, gold, gilded copper and shell.

Maker unknown, vessel with condor and human head, 400–1000, Peru, Tiwanaku style, pottery.

Tumi (knife) with condor, Moche, 200–800, copper, shell, turquoise.

Ian Rees, *Andean Condor in Flight*, 2025, colour pencil on Bristol Paper.

Nazca lines showing a condor, 200 BCE–500 CE Peru, geoglyphs made in the soil.

bird, a rock on the temple floor was carved in the form of the condor's head and neck; it has been speculated that the head was used as a sacrificial altar.

A controversial ritual is performed in many Peruvian villages during the Yawar Fiesta or Blood Festival, in which a captured condor is adorned with pennants and paraded through the streets by its wingtips. The bird is then tied onto the back of a bull, pecking and clawing at it while bullfighters kill the bull (generally, the condor survives and is set free). In this essentially European-imported ritual, the bull represents the Spanish colonists killed by the villagers, who are assisted by the condor, representing the Andean people.

The Andean condor remains an emblem of power and is the national symbol of many South American countries, appearing on flags, stamps, coins and banknotes. Yet despite such regard, the bird is threatened with extinction through habitat loss, pesticides and hunting. Captive breeding programmes have been established in several countries to help offset the loss.

GRASSLAND & SAVANNA

Found only in New Zealand, the flightless and nocturnal kiwi is one of the planet's most unusual birds, its body resembling the eponymous fruit, clothed in hairlike feathers and sporting heavy whiskers and short, stout legs. Its awl-like bill bears nostrils at the tip, with which it probes the soil for prey.

The Māori settlers who arrived in New Zealand from Polynesia by canoe around the thirteenth century associated the kiwi with Tāne-mahuta, god of the forest and creator of plants and birds, and considered the bird to fall under his care. According to tradition, the kiwi was Tāne-mahuta's eldest child and offers protection to humans (also relatives of the god) as their elder brothers and sisters.

For more than a thousand years the Māori hunted the kiwi sustainably, recognizing each of the five species and giving them names. Special chants and rituals would take place before setting off for the hunt, acknowledging that the bird enjoyed Tāne-mahuta's special protection. Kiwi meat was considered fit for chiefs, with the birds preserved in fat and steamed in a traditional method of cooking known as *hāngī*, which used heated rocks buried in a pit oven. Their feathers were used to craft ceremonial cloaks called *kahu kiwi*, with white albino ones especially prized.

The first Europeans to arrive in New Zealand regarded the kiwi as unusual, more like a mammal than a bird. A skin was taken to England in 1812, inspiring the first

Johannes Gerardus Keulemans, '*Apteryx mantelli*' (North-Island Kiw) i, 1888, from *A History of the Birds of New Zealand* by Walter Lawry Buller.

Peter Wilson, *Big Hand in the Sky*, 1978, oil on canvas.

illustration of the bird, which portrayed it more like a penguin. The first living bird, sent to Britain in 1851 as a specimen for London Zoo, attracted much attention because of its unusual appearance.

Under the 1840 Treaty of Waitangi, signed between the British Crown and the Māori tribes, the Māori were granted guardianship over the kiwi, considered by them to be *taonga*, or treasure. Every bird under Māori care is celebrated on release, with children singing special songs and tribal elders formally welcoming the birds to their new home with blessings and hopes for a safe future.

However, fine Māori cloaks drew the attention of the Europeans, resulting in exploitation of the kiwi's plumage for fashion accessories, including scarves and muffs, and tied flies for fishing. Unrelenting pressure on the bird's numbers saw a marked decline: once estimated at around 12 million, by 1998 the population had plummeted to fewer than 100,000 birds, and by 2008 it had fallen even further to about 70,000. Today it is estimated that around 68,000 kiwis remain, and unmanaged populations continue to decline by 2 per cent every year. Happily, in areas where kiwis are managed the situation is improving, with many populations stable or increasing.

Today the kiwi is widely recognized as New Zealand's emblem, the association proving so strong that the term 'Kiwi' is used internationally as a colloquial name for New Zealanders. It is a frequent character in popular culture, for instance in the Christmas song 'Sticky Beak the Kiwi', first recorded in 1961, where a kiwi insists on pulling Santa's sleigh when delivering presents south of the equator. Alwyn Owen's 1963 fable *How the Kiwi Lost its Wings* incorporates the Māori mythology of Tāne-mahuta along with white feathers, a symbol of cowardice during the First World War, in an origin story to explain the features of the iconic New Zealand bird. The story has been published as a book, made into an animated film, set to music for the Auckland Philharmonic as *Tāne and the Kiwi*, and performed as a ballet by the Royal New Zealand Ballet. There must be few other occasions when an indigenous myth or legend has made a bird into a national and international icon and helped shape its survival.

With its eerie cries, dark plumage and arrow-like appearance, along with unusual habits such as ascending into the sky at dusk and never landing except to breed, it is not surprising that the common swift (*Apus apus*) has puzzled humankind over the centuries, often being associated with the supernatural.

Like the adjective, the English vernacular name swift derives from the Old English word *swifan*, which means moving fast. The bird is often confused with its more famous (and more numerous) cousin the swallow, largely as a result of centuries-old translations of the Bible. Pliny clearly recognized the distinction, and in his *Natural History* called the swift *apus* (literally 'the footless one', from the Greek *a*, without, and *pous*, foot), the same name scientists would adopt for the bird nearly two millennia later.

The misconception that swifts had no feet at all was widespread, arising from the length of time they spend in the air and their diminutive legs. In heraldry, the bird (known as the martlet) was shown without feet and symbolized a noble family's fourth son with no land to inherit, a situation summed up by the Reverend Charles Swainson in 1885, who lamented of 'the bird that lacketh feet wherewith to settle upon land, and they lacking land whereon to set their feet'.

In English folklore, the swift was thought to be legless and to hibernate in mud, its scream signalling the departure of the dead for hell, making it a bird of ill omen; some older English words used for the birds include devil-bird, deviling, swingdevil, devil's screecher and devil swallow. In Shakespeare's *Macbeth* (Act 1, scene 6), Banquo mistakenly identifies the swift as a good omen when spotting it outside Macbeth's castle shortly before Duncan is killed:

This guest of summer,
The temple-haunting martlet, does approve,
By his loved mansionry, that the heaven's breath
Smells wooingly here. No jutty, frieze,
Buttress, nor coign of vantage, but this bird
Hath made his pendant bed and procreant cradle.
Where they most breed and haunt, I have observed,
The air is delicate.

In the northeast of Scotland, the common swift was believed to bring bad luck to river fishermen, while farmers in the southern counties of England were encouraged to shoot them as they were held to be 'regular limbs of Satan'. One farmer is said to have shot seventeen of the birds, losing seventeen of his finest cows some seven weeks later. In Wales, the swift is a predictor of the weather: if it feeds high up in the air the weather is settled for fair, while if it feeds low down, rain is approaching. Its screaming is supposed to indicate a change of conditions from fair to rainy.

The indigenous Ainu people of Japan believed that the common swift lived in heaven and descended to the earth in the summer to play, returning each night. The birds' skin and heads were treasured and thought to bring good luck. Dances performed in the Hokkaido municipality of Biratori are inspired by the birds. The traditional *Chak piyak* dance captures swifts in flight after the rains, accompanied by singing traditionally led by women, with an emphasis on voice effects and rhythm.

Beijing is known as the swift capital (Yanjing). Beijing swifts (*Apus apus pekinensis*, a subspecies of the common swift) became synonymous with the Chinese capital around 1417, when they began to breed in the city's gatehouses.

Giovanni Bellini, (workshop of), *Madonna and Child* (detail), *c.* 1510, oil on wood.

Archibald Thorburn, *Swift* (detail), *c.* 1915, watercolour and bodycolour over pencil on paper.

The birds migrate to the region twice a year from Africa, crossing some twenty borders and covering around 26,000 km (16,000 miles) there and back.

The close relationship the people of China formed with the swift dates back to the Neolithic period and is embedded in the mythology of the nation as the 'Black Bird' of the Yin and Shang dynasties and the 'Hu Yan' in the Song and Ming dynasties. In Chinese traditional literature, God sent the swift down to the world and gave birth to Jiandi, the mother of Kie, founder of the Shang dynasty. In an alternative story, the 'Odes of Shanga' tell of Jiandi, the second wife of Emperor Ku, who swallowed an egg dropped by a black bird (thought to be a swift) and miraculously gave birth to Xie, reported to have helped the legendary king Yu the Great to control the Great Flood.

Swifts spend more time in the air than any other bird and can sleep on the wing, with some species remaining airborne for up to 200 days. Edward Thomas's poem 'Haymaking' (1917) captures the essence of this extraordinary bird, as free as the wind:

While over them shrill shrieked in his fierce glee
The swift with wings and tail as sharp and narrow
As if the bow had flown off with the arrow.

Most people in Britain and Ireland are pleased to see the arrival of swifts each year, the birds heralding the beginning of summer and the good weather it brings. However, the epic journey they undertake was only understood in fairly recent times. Edward Jenner, inventor of vaccination, was convinced that the birds migrated at a time when some still thought they simply disappeared into mud or ponds for the winter. Around the 1760s, he marked some swifts by cutting off their toes and found that they returned to the same place to breed in a fattened and healthy condition; as a result, he was more certain than ever that his theory of migration was correct.

❖ Bruno Liljefors, *Common Swifts*, 1886, oil on canvas.

✻ Vincent van Gogh, *Four Swifts with Landscape Sketches Paris, April–September 1887*, 1887, pencil, pen, ink and chalk on paper.

✻

HORNBILLS

FAMILY Bucerotidae

Like toucans, the distinctive anatomy of hornbills has attracted sustained attention in both science and legend, with long, down-curved and frequently brightly coloured bills and sometimes a horny casque on their upper mandible. With long eyelashes, a crown of mohican-like feathers, wrinkled facial skin and swollen wattles, some species can present quite the clownish look.

There are fifty-five species of hornbill, occupying tropical and subtropical Africa and Asia. They are the only birds in the world whose atlas and axis vertebrae are fused together, thought to provide support for their unusual bills. The casques in most species are very light, largely filled with air, and can serve to amplify the bird's calls. An exception is the helmeted hornbill (*Rhinoplax vigil*), where the casque is solid, often used in aerial jousts. Sometimes known as 'hornbill ivory', it is used as a carving material in Japan and particularly China, where it is considered more valuable even than jade, and in India the birds are hunted for it.

Owing to the diversity of species found there, the Malaysian state of Sarawak is nicknamed the 'land of the hornbills' and its indigenous people regard the birds as sacred symbols of strength, protection and spirituality. They are connected to one of the most powerful gods of the Iban people, Singalang Burong, the god of war, a portentous bird associated with visions, prophecies and justice. The rhinoceros hornbill (*Buceros rhinoceros*) is known as the king of the worldly birds, acting as an intermediary between man and god, while the helmeted hornbill (*Rhinoplax vigil*) guards the passage between life and the afterlife to judge the worth of those who pass.

The Dayaks of Borneo carved stunning wooden sculptures of rhinoceros hornbills for use in the ritual of headhunting (taking the heads of their enemies). The largest of these sculptures were placed atop tall posts to enable their spirits to obtain favours from Singalang Burong. Many of these indigenous people use the two long central tail feathers of hornbills to adorn ceremonial attire and weapons at weddings, funerals and other official functions, while their meat and skulls are taken for medicinal purposes.

Elsewhere in Southeast Asia, the raucous call of the great hornbill (*Buceros bicornis*) signals the presence of ancestral spirits and guides hunters on their quests. In Thailand, it is revered as a symbol of eternal love and devotion, as the birds form lifelong bonds with their mates and engage in elaborate courtship rituals. The kampilan, a traditional sword of Muslims (Moros) in the Philippines, has a unique bifurcated hilt believed to represent the gaping mouth of either the mythical naga (serpent) or crocodile, or perhaps a hornbill or cockatoo. In Papua New Guinea, casques from the Blyth's hornbill (*Rhyticeros plicatus*) are worn as phallic shields, while their lower mandible provides spear points, often proving lethal weapons.

For tribal communities in northeast India and southwest China, the cultural significance of hornbills is intertwined with traditional art and rituals. Intricate hornbill motifs adorn ceremonial masks and tribal regalia, reflecting the bird's revered status as a symbol of prosperity and protection. The feathers and double-pronged casque of the great hornbill hold particular cultural significance for the Naga people and are often incorporated into their ceremonial attire, while the bird's flesh is believed to be of medicinal value. Marking their respect for nature, certain Naga tribes observed the Angami Sekrenyi or Festival of Purification, a period during which hunting was prohibited to allow the hornbills and other wildlife to breed undisturbed.

During the migratory season, the Mishmi and Adi people shoot fifty to seventy wreathed hornbills (*Rhyticeros undulatus*) for meat and to use the gizzards as medicine to cure stomach problems, the feathers to decorate homes and the casques to adorn headgear. In contrast, the Sema Nagas avoid eating flesh and vegetables when dancing with hornbill feathers, believing them to cause sores on the feet. Some tribes hold the wreathed hornbill to be the guide of dead souls to the lower world. The annual Hornbill Festival in Nagaland is named after the bird as a symbol of respect.

'*Buceros rhinoceros*' (Rhinoceros Hornbill), 1816–30, from *Dictionnaire des Sciences Naturelles. Planches 2e partie: Règne Organisé. Zoologie. Ornithologie* by M. Dumont de Sainte-Croix.

Mansur, 'Great Hornbill' (detail), *c.* 1615–20, folio from the Shah Jahan Album, ink, opaque watercolour and gold on paper.

Some African myths, superstitions and fables treat ground hornbills as bringers of rain, good fortune or hope, while others consider them omens of death. The Zulu associate the southern ground hornbill (*Bucorvus leadbeateri*) with faith, reflecting its tendency to look to the heavens in times of famine and hardship. In Zulu, the bird is called *umkolwana* or 'believer', and killing a hornbill is treated as a serious sin which could bring disease to cattle or wash away lands. To the north, the southern yellow-billed hornbill (*Tockus leucomelas*) is also regarded as a symbol of faith, specifically in a better tomorrow.

As well as harbingers of rain, hornbills are considered accurate predictors of prosperity, and their feeding spots are thought to be the best places to raise cattle. The Yoruba in Nigeria see the bird as a messenger between

Maker unknown, hornbill-head-shaped throwing knife, Cameroon, Africa, n.d., iron, wood.

Utagawa Hiroshige, *Purple Magnolia and Hornbill*, c. 1830, woodblock print, ink and colour on paper.

Gordon Deacon, *Hornbills*, c. 1934, colour relief print.

the gods and humans, carrying prayers and blessings on its wings, and its presence is believed to bring good fortune and protection to those who honour the natural world. In other traditions, hornbills are killed for ritual purposes, for example during times of drought. With the bird's renowned odour, it was thought that the water gods would bring rain to cleanse a river if a ritualistically killed hornbill is placed there. In another fable, the hornbill warns of the dangers of adultery.

Hornbill casques are often procured in West Africa for their medicinal properties and to protect against witchcraft. In tribal celebrations, carved replicas of their beaked heads are used as part of costumes worn for dances, performed in the belief that the hornbill conveyed the souls of the dead to the underworld.

The most widespread species of swallow, the well-loved barn swallow (*Hirundo rustica*) is one of the most accomplished fliers of the bird world. It has forged a harmonious relationship with humankind, its return to the northern hemisphere each spring signifying hope and change, though sometimes also provoking suspicion.

Swallows are often found in ancient Egyptian art, though individual species can rarely be identified. One exception is a funerary papyrus showing a barn swallow perched on the prow of the sun god Ra-Horakhty's boat as he journeys through the night, there to greet the sun and proclaim the approach of dawn. Swallows are also depicted on top of mounds in Egyptian tombs and papyri, thought to represent the first areas of earth to emerge from the primeval waters.

A wall painting on the Greek island of Santorini by an artist of the Bronze Age Minoan civilization depicts a spring scene, with a pair of swallows among lotus flowers. Some observers believe that the birds are 'kissing', while others take them to be two fighting males. In ancient Greece and across much of Europe, for a barn swallow to nest on one's property was considered a token of good luck, and to prevent ill fortune falling on a home some Greeks would capture the birds, anointing them with oil before releasing them on their journey.

For Christians, the swallow's advent each spring made it a symbol of the Resurrection, and it appears as an incarnation of Christ in

John James Audubon, '*Hirundo rustica*' (Barn or Chimney Swallow), no. 10, pl. 48, 1840, from *The Birds of America*, vol 1.

Artist unknown, room of lilies or spring, Akrotiri fresco, Thera (Santorini), Minoan Civilization, sixteenth century BCE.

Carlo Crivelli, *The Madonna of the Swallow* (detail), *c.* 1490, tempera and gold on wood.

Renaissance scenes of the Annunciation or the Nativity, nestled in holes or under eaves, for example in Carlo Crivelli's *Madonna of the Swallow* (*c.* 1490), where it perches on top of the Virgin's throne. Like the goldfinch and the robin, the swallow was said to have attempted to remove the crown of thorns from Christ's head during the Crucifixion and pricked itself, resulting in the red patch of feathers on the bird's throat and forehead when marked with his blood. It was also thought to have comforted Christ on the Cross with its singing.

Swallows were often endowed with supernatural powers: it was said that they sensed where foul acts had been committed and would not nest on a house whose inhabitants were known for cruelty. A passing representation of the bird appears in a medieval Anglo-French manuscript of the apocryphal Book of Tobit. The scene shows Tobit losing his eyesight, illustrating the verse: 'And as he was sleeping, hot dung out of a swallow's nest fell upon his eyes, and he was made blind' (2:11).

The swallow is attributed with countless superstitions in European folklore. To damage its nest or take its eggs was thought to lead to cows producing no milk or hens ceasing to lay, while if a swallow fell down the chimney of a house it foretold the death of an inhabitant; if it alighted on someone their death would swiftly follow. In the English county of Norfolk, death was again foreseen if many swallows gathered on the roof of a house, the departing spirit thought to fly off with the birds. If swallows gathered on the roof of a church, it was said that they were discussing who would die before they returned in the spring. In Ireland, the swallow was considered one of the devil's birds.

Traditional medicine made use of swallows for treating ailments. In *The Homish Apothecary* of the mid-1500s, a swallow's nest is proposed as a cure for those 'that have quinsy [an abscess] in the throat', while consuming crushed swallow broth was once thought to cure the uncontrollable motions of epilepsy and stammering through sympathetic magic. A seventeenth-century recipe in *Mistress Jane Hussey's Still-Room Book* called for forty to fifty swallows to be placed alive in a mortar and pounded to make a potion to 'comforteth the brain', while ingesting a swallow's heart was said to cure drunkenness and the bite of a bad dog.

The barn swallow and its relatives enjoy a mixed reputation in Native American folklore. In one myth it stole fire from the sun and brought it back to earth, at which a wrathful god hurled a fire brand at the swallow, burning its tail feathers and leaving its emblematic forked tail. But like other small birds, swallows sometimes appear in folktales to represent humility and industriousness. Some Southwestern tribes like the Zuni associate them with rain, while in Hopi myth the swallow brings corn kernels to their starving people. The Chippewa name

Giacomo Balla, *Swallows Flying*, 1913, oil on canvas.

Itō Jakuchū, *Swallow and Camellia*, c. 1900, woodblock print.

for the bird is *Shau-shau'-wun-ni-bi-sence*, 'little bird that tumbles over and over in the air'. The Inuit considered swallows to be the spirits of children and believed that when they returned to the nest, they were recalling childish joys. Even today, children like to watch swallows building their *iglviaks* (miniature igloos).

In Japan, swallows are revered for their connection to the changing seasons, with their arrival in spring heralding renewal and new beginnings. A proverb that translates as 'the barn swallow blooms' is used to celebrate personal growth and maturation. The swallow holds a special place in Chinese culture too, considered a symbol of good luck and prosperity. To explain their disappearance in the winter, the birds are said to transform into mussels by the sea.

The imaginations of previous generations were ever exercised by the mystery of birds' migration, with many suggesting that they hibernated in pond mud or holes in the ground until spring. In the verse 'To A. L., Persuasions to Love', seventeenth-century poet Thomas Carew was unequivocal in his belief that 'Like swallows, when your summer's done, / They'll fly, and seek some warmer sun', but it was only at the end of the nineteenth century that ornithologists agreed that swallows and other summer visitors to the northern hemisphere migrated to southern lands for the winter. Since then, their immense journeys have been well observed, and the swallow is a popular tattoo motif among sailors, marking a safe return. A mariner would be tattooed with this fellow wanderer after sailing 5,000 nautical miles, and a second swallow would be added on reaching 10,000 miles.

Félix Henri Bracquemond, *The Swallows*, c. 1881, pen, brush and black ink, with black chalk, graphite and touches of black Conté crayon on tan wove paper.

A group of birds in the *Meropidae* family, both sexes of bee-eaters have exotic plumage, slender bodies and usually elongated tail feathers. Across indigenous traditions, the bird is often depicted as a symbol of agility, grace and adaptability, embodying qualities that resonate with the cultural heritage of local communities.

With three genera and thirty species, bee-eaters are mostly found in Africa and Asia, with a few in southern Europe, Australia and New Guinea. All possess long, downturned bills and medium to long wings. They have been depicted on the postage stamps of at least thirty-eight countries, with the European bee-eater (*Merops apiaster*) and the southern carmine bee-eater (*Merops nubicoides*) the most common subjects.

For such colourful birds, depictions of bee-eaters in classical art are rare. The only known example from ancient Egypt is a relief, probably of a little green bee-eater (*Merops orientalis*), on a wall of the mortuary temple of Queen Hatshepsut at Deir el-Bahari. The Egyptians believed that bee-eaters possessed medicinal properties, prescribing the application of their fat to deter biting flies and treating eyes with smoke from charred bee-eater legs to cure an unspecified female complaint. Blue-cheeked bee-eaters (*Merops persicus*) appear on an early Roman mural discovered in the villa of Agrippina.

In Greek mythology, the Theban Botres was killed by his father when he desecrated a ritual sacrifice of a ram to the god Apollo by tasting the animal's brains. Taking pity on him, the gods turned him into the bird Aeropus, a bee-eater. Aristotle observed that bee-eaters nested in tunnels and that nesting adults were fed by their previous offspring, while Virgil advised beekeepers to kill the birds to protect their apiaries. The Roman author Aelian recorded a belief that the bird flew backwards, with its gaze turned behind, likely a reference to the bee-eater's habit of hovering.

For Hindus, the bee-eater is associated with archery and archer gods; the shape of the bird when in flight being thought to resemble a bow, with its long bill as an arrow (its name in Sanskrit means 'Vishnu's bow'). It was believed that rumour-mongers were reincarnated as bee-eaters, because of the poison the birds bore

John Gould, '*Merops apiaster*' (European Bee-eater), 1837, from *Birds of Europe*, vol. II.

Mughal school, *Bee-eater*, nineteenth century, from the Kevorkian album, opaque watercolour and gold on paper.

in their beaks from bees (it had clearly not been observed that the bird in fact thrashes its beak until the poison sac is excised). A beautiful depiction of a bee-eater appears in a miniature from a nineteenth-century Mughal manuscript.

With seven different species found in Tanzania, bee-eaters hold cultural significance in its folklore, with their vibrant colours held to represent vitality and renewal. Traditional stories and narratives reflect their enduring influence as revered creatures who embody the spirit of the grasslands and the natural world.

Native to Europe and Asia, the house sparrow (*Passer domesticus*) is now the most widespread wild bird, found on every continent except Antarctica. Its familiarity seems to have bred contempt across the ages, with the bird variously being linked to human attachment, lasciviousness, lowliness, melancholy and pugnacity.

The sparrow was sacred to the Greek goddess of love, Aphrodite, and her Roman counterpart, Venus. In his *Parlement of Foules*, Chaucer calls it 'Venus' son', possibly in reference to the bird's fecundity and the belief that its eggs were an aphrodisiac. Later, in the Prologue to the *Canterbury Tales*, he includes a description of the Summoner (a man who called people before the ecclesiastical court for their spiritual crimes) as 'hot he was, and lecherous as a sparrow'.

John Donne keeps the romantic associations but treads more delicately in his poem 'An Epithalamion, or Marriage Song on the Lady Elizabeth and Count Palatine being Married on St Valentine's Day' (1613), writing of 'The sparrow that neglects his life for love'. In other works, both Chaucer and Donne cite a legend that if a girl saw a sparrow on St Valentine's Day, it meant that she would marry a farmer or a poor man but would be happy. In Shakespeare's *Measure for Measure* (Act 3, scene 2), Lucio criticizes the harsh policy of abstinence ordered by the duke, complaining: 'This ungenitur'd agent will unpeople the province with continency; sparrows must not build in his house-eves because they are lecherous.'

Sparrows were often viewed as predictors of weather conditions. In his companion works 'Phenomena' and 'Weather Signs', the Greek poet Aratus noted signs warning of the arrival of a pending gale, later taken up by English country folk in the saying: 'When sparrows ceaseless chirp at dawn of day / And in their holes the wren and robin stay.' The eighteenth-century English poet Stephen Duck also noted in 'The Thresher's Labour' that twittering birds took cover from oncoming rain:

But, on a sudden, if a Storm appears,
Their chirping Noise no longer dins your Ears:
They fly for Shelter to the thickest Bush;
There silent sit, and All at once is hush.

The English Bible includes many references to the house sparrow, considering it as a symbol of the lowliest of people, who were nevertheless

Edward Poynter, *Lesbia and her Sparrow* (detail), 1907, oil on canvas.

John Gould, '*Passer domesticus*' (Common or House-Sparrow), 1873, from *The Birds of Great Britain*.

under God's protection: 'Are not five sparrows sold for two farthings, and not one of them is forgotten before God?' (Luke 12:6). The reference is echoed in Shakespeare's *Hamlet* (Act 5, scene 2), when the eponymous prince finally realises that he cannot defy fate or God's will, acknowledging that 'there's special providence in the fall of a sparrow', and that all living things, including himself, are destined to die.

According to Christian legend, birds were said to attempt to divert soldiers from finding where Jesus was praying in the Garden of Gethsemane. The exception was the sparrow, whose constant chattering warned of his whereabouts. As a consequence, Jesus cursed sparrows and decreed that their flesh would be unclean. Another story tells that while Christ was being crucified on the Cross, the sparrows maliciously chirped 'He is living, He is living!' to urge his tormenters to fresh cruelties, while swallows cried with the opposite intent, 'Dead! Dead!' As a result, the swallow is blessed while

the sparrow suffers another curse and, for its sin, hops ever since, because invisible bonds tie its legs together.

A particularly compelling story from Anglo-Saxon times involved the siege of the English town of Cirencester in the eighth century, where lighted matches were attached to sparrows to ignite their nests and fire the town, which took on the name Sparrowcester. In later times, it was believed in many parts of Britain that if a sparrow was caught, it had to be killed immediately, or the catcher would die. It was also considered a bad omen for a sparrow to tap a window, as this portended death in the family.

The 'Sparwe cok' and 'sparwe hen' are pictured in the early fifteenth-century Sherborne Missal, recorded as spreading in numbers with expanding agriculture and urbanisation. The bird soon became regarded as a pest and in a bid to control its numbers, farmers sent boys into the fields with bows and arrows and instructed them to create 'much clamour'. Sometimes, sparrow charms were used to ward off the birds from fields: in one remarkable attempt sowers placed three grains of corn under their tongues and, at the end of a furrow, spat them out as a benediction was uttered: 'No sparrow will come into the field, although the neighbouring one be full of sparrows.' Another method to deny the sparrow's thievery of corn stored in a barn was to place a bone from a grave at the building's entrance.

Despite its pestilence, the sparrow was long used as a food item. Though Andrew Boorde in his *Dyetry of Health* (1547) found sparrows 'hard of digestion', a delicious broth of sparrows was especially popular among Elizabethans as a winter dish, along with sparrow pie.

Maker unknown, relief with the seer Calchas (sparrow, top right corner), relief 140–160 CE and head 170–190 CE, marble.

John Siferwas and others, marginal decoration, including a male house sparrow and female house sparrow, *c.* 1399–1407, from the Sherborne Missal.

Artist unknown, Garden Fresco from the House of the Golden Bracelet (sparrow top centre), Pompeii, first century CE, water-based pigments on limestone plaster.

Like Eastern emperors, the male common pheasant (*Phasianus colchicus colchicus*) and ring-necked pheasant (*Phasianus colchicus torquatus*) swagger across northern landscapes, their finery totally at odds with their surroundings. Long prized for their meat as the most hunted game bird, they are also symbols of luxury and maternal love.

Native to Asia, both species were imported to Europe and then to North America as domesticated fowls, thereby conquering the Western world. They have inspired many artists to plaster their palettes with scarlet, gold, fiery copper red, chestnut brown, bottle green and iridescent purple, white or cream and black, though few have captured their spectacular appearance quite as well as the Scottish artist Archibald Thorburn. Yet many birders consider the pheasant an invader and expunged it from their life lists as late as the end of the twentieth century.

In Chinese mythology pheasants, including the ring-necked pheasant, are sometimes interchanged with the legendary phoenix as emblems of beauty and good fortune. In some tales it is a bird of ill omen – if it did not call in the twelfth lunar month, floods would follow – and is believed to turn into an oyster or a snake during the winter. Other associations are with seduction and extramarital affairs, possibly because the male pheasant has a harem. The mythological Vermilion Bird, a spirit creature of the Chinese constellations, resembles a pheasant, with its five-coloured plumage perpetually covered in flames.

Despite being quite widespread in the Western world, few legends are attached to the bird. The common pheasant is first found in Greek mythology when Jason brought the birds from the river Phasis in the ancient land of Colchis (modern-day Georgia), following his search for the Golden Fleece. A Roman mosaic floor in Tunisia shows a pheasant standing between two shrubs, while on the magnificent mosaic pavement from the Basilica of Justinian in Sabratha, Libya, a large, brightly coloured pheasant stalks around the grapevines above a peacock in profile.

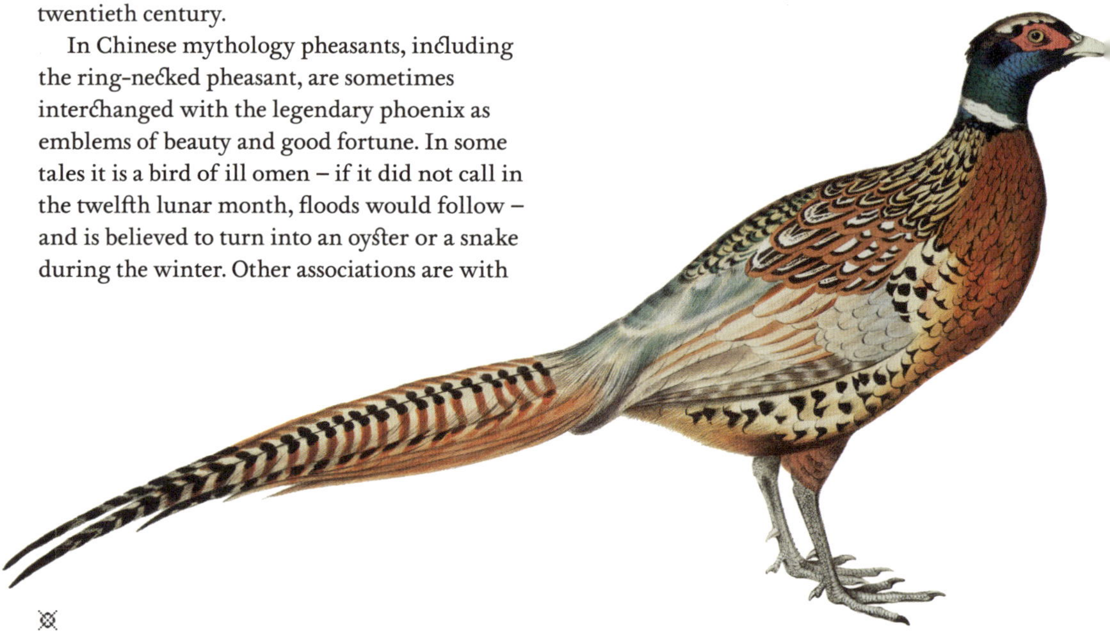

John Edward Grey, *'Phasianus torquatus'* (Chinese Ring-necked Pheasant), 1830–34, from *Illustrations of Indian Zoology*.

Male pheasant in the Lovell Lectionary, *c.* 1400–10, from southern England, illuminated manuscript.

The Caucasian or 'Old English' pheasant was introduced to Europe perhaps by Alexander the Great, and during Roman times to Britain, where it was reared as a domestic fowl. Later, the Normans introduced the Chinese ring-necked pheasant, and both quickly became well established as a luxury food item at court. Over time, the ring-necked hybridized with the pure English variety, with the result that nearly all pheasants today have some trace of a white collar.

Captivity in the poultry yard seems to have been the bird's lot for the next few centuries. Evidence of clergy rearing the bird is found in a passable illustration of a male pheasant in the medieval Lovell Lectionary, though the colour of the body and neck is a major detraction, more in line with that of a peahen. It also appears in the Sherborne Missal, yet early illustrated manuscripts and dictionaries reveal that the pheasant was neither well known nor feral in Britain before the fourteenth century. Further introductions of the Chinese 'white neck-ringed' variety came in the eighteenth century, and by the early nineteenth century they had become a primary game bird.

The long and tapering tail feathers of the pheasant have been greatly prized in Britain and there is an established country tradition of wearing those of the cock bird in the hat band, made famous by the legendary Robin Hood. Longer pheasant tails are customarily used in decorative arrangements or as large and showy headdresses for carnivals and dances. In both

Britain and North America, many artificial angling lures for fly-fishing are made of pheasants' feathers because they are so colourful.

Although pheasants came late to North America, Native Americans consider them a symbol of protection and concealment, having observed that the birds spend most of their time hunkered down in tall grass, shielded from sight and nesting on the ground rather than shrubs or trees. Some tribes, such as the Cherokee, went on to develop dances that involve the bird.

Pheasants appear sensitive to unusual sounds and vibrations, and in some parts of the world it is claimed they provide early warning alarms. In Britain during the First World War pheasants were used as sentinels to warn against Zeppelin attacks, sensing bomb explosions as the airships approached. It is also said that pheasants in Kent on the English Channel made agitated calls during the evacuations of Dunkirk in 1940.

❖ Photographer unknown, *Ring-necked Pheasants Feeding in the Snow*, c. 1900, Keystone View Co., hand-coloured gelatin silver print.

✻ John J. Eyers, *Hanging Game Birds (Pheasant)*, 1872, oil on canvas.

J. J. Eyers, 1672

*

The kakapo (*Strigops habroptila*), sometimes called the owl parrot, night parrot or moss chicken, is a large, ground-dwelling, nocturnal parrot endemic to New Zealand. A flightless bird, it is unique for its owl-like face, forward-looking eyes, large beak and short wings, tail and legs.

The kakapo features prominently in Māori mythology, rituals and beliefs, with folklore suggesting that it was present throughout New Zealand when Polynesian cultures first arrived in the country around 700 years ago. The bird's irregular breeding cycle was understood to be associated with the heavy fruiting or 'masting' events of the evergreen coniferous rimu tree (*Dacrydium cupressinum*), which took place every two to four years. This led the Māori to credit the bird with the ability to prophesy the future. The belief was supported by observations of the kakapo dropping the ripened berries of the hinau and tawa trees into sheltered pools of water to preserve them as a food supply for the forthcoming summer, which accounts for the current Māori practice of immersing food in water.

According to Māori legend, the toroa or wandering albatross (*Diomedea epomophora*) was once a land bird. However, because its brilliant white plumage made it vulnerable on land, it swapped places with the kakapo, once a seabird, and soared out to sea, its markings matching the foaming swells of the ocean. In the meantime, the kakapo vanished into the twilight of the forest, its mossy green plumage blending in with its new home. Until the arrival of humans, it remained so safe in the depths of the bush that it eventually lost its ability to fly.

An elaboration of this legend held that the kakapo and toroa argued over which one of them should rule the land. They agreed to take turns trying to hide from each other, the one who best camouflaged themselves proving the winner. The toroa first tried to hide in open land, but his bright white plumage meant that the kakapo found him easy to spot. When it was the kakapo's turn, it crouched under some ferns and blended in so well that the toroa searched in vain until the kakapo began to laugh. Ever since, the albatross has been flying over the wide ocean, while the kakapo lives on land, blending in with the colours of the forest.

The Māori considered the meat of the kakapo a delicacy and, when the bird was widespread, hunted it for food. Cooking was done in underground steam ovens or in gourds of boiling oil. The flesh of the bird was stored in containers, with bundles of kakapo tail feathers decorating their sides as a means of identifying their contents.

As well as eating the meat, the Māori would use the birds' skins with the beautiful green and brown feathers still attached or individually weave in feathers with flax fibre to make cloaks and capes for high-born people, each one requiring up to 11,000 feathers. These garments were highly valued, and those still in existence today are considered *taonga* or treasure; an old Māori adage, 'You have a kakapo cape and still you complain of the cold', describes someone who is never satisfied. Kakapo feathers were also used to decorate the heads of *taiaha*, a traditional close-quarters staff weapon made from either wood or whalebone and used with short, sharp strikes or stabbing thrusts. The feathers were removed before the weapon was taken into combat.

Kakapos were regarded as affectionate pets by both Māori and European settlers, with the British soldier George Grey writing in the nineteenth century that his kakapo's behaviour was 'more like that of a dog than a bird'. Although kakapo numbers were reduced by Māori settlement, they declined much more rapidly after European colonization, and the bird is now critically endangered.

Johannes Gerardus Keulemans, '*Strigops habroptilus*' (Kakapo), *c.* 1888, from *A History of the Birds of New Zealand* by Walter Lawry Buller.

※ Maker unknown, *Taiaha kura* (long handled striking weapon) from New Zealand, 1750–1850, wood, feathers, dog hair, pāua (abalone shell), woodcarving.

❖ Maker unknown, the *kahu kākāpō* after conservation and mounting, *c.* 1810s–20s, *whatu kākahu* (cloak weaving) with kakapo feathers, processed flax fibre and European wool.

※

With cinnamon-pink bodies, zebra-striped wings, raised crest like a Chinese fan and a rapier-like bill, the Eurasian hoopoe is a distinctive bird with widespread cultural significance. It is found across Europe, Asia and northern Africa as a migrant or resident.

Hoopoes were considered sacred in Minoan Crete and ancient Egypt, often appearing on temple walls and tombs, and the bird was used in the Old Kingdom as a symbolic hieroglyphic code to show that the child was the rightful heir to the father. The Egyptians believed migratory birds were reborn souls of the dead, and a watercolour by the famous archaeologist Howard Carter copies an image, originally painted on the tomb of Khnumhotep II at Beni Hasan, of a hoopoe sitting in an acacia tree, symbol of eternity.

The bird was also considered to represent gratitude, as hoopoes repaid their ageing parents by trimming their wings, licking the mist off their eyes and bringing them food as they acquired new plumage. The behaviour was noted by later commentators such as Pliny and St Isidore of Seville, who identified the hoopoe as one of just a handful of animals to treat their elders with sympathy when they became feeble, as depicted in some medieval bestiaries showing offspring plucking at the feathers of a parent.

In the folklore of the eastern Mediterranean, the hoopoe was frequently associated with kingship, wisdom and devotion. It appears in the Qur'an (Sura 27:31) as the messenger of King Solomon, portrayed as a great and wealthy king who reigned over nature and demons. Believing that the Queen of Sheba worships the sun instead of God, Solomon sends her a letter

⊠ Artist unknown, Queen of Sheba and hoopoe, Safavid dynasty, *c.* 1590–1600, ink, opaque watercolour and gold on paper.

⁂ John Gould, '*Upupa epops*' (Hoopoe), 1873, from *The Birds of Great Britain*, vol. I.

via his hoopoe (*hiudad*) messenger, calling her to come to him 'in humble submission', to which the queen responds with gifts and a message before setting off to visit him. The moment when the hoopoe returns the queen's message to Solomon, along with angels bearing her gifts, is portrayed in a seventeenth-century painting from the Mughal empire. The king sits on a richly adorned throne, linking his prowess as the ideal just and wise ruler with that of a Mughal emperor.

In the epic poem *The Conference of the Birds* by the Persian poet Attar of Nishapur (1177), the world's birds gather to decide who is to be their sovereign. The hoopoe, wisest of them all, proposes they find the legendary Simurgh (a benevolent bird in Persian mythology) and leads the birds, each of whom represents a human fault that prevents people from attaining enlightenment. Only thirty birds complete the journey, realizing that they themselves are the Simurgh they have sought, the poem teaching that the aim of life's quest is the discovery of the divine within.

In much of the Arab world the hoopoe is called the doctor, its head believed to be an indispensable ingredient in charms and the practice of witchcraft. The blood and heart were used in folk medicine, and the blood was said to be a powerful 'ink' for writing spells. The bird is also considered a water-finder, a virtue that endeared it to Solomon and is particularly appreciated by those who dwell in the desert, while its unique 'hoop-hoop-hoop' vocalizations signalled danger or alerted people to potential threats.

The hoopoe's flesh exudes an offensive smell, especially strong about its nest. This may explain associated legends suggesting it guarded treasures in its nest and was entrusted with transporting the *shamir*, the miraculous worm or substance that could split the stones of the Temple, the use of any iron tool having been expressly prohibited (Deuteronomy 27:5, Hul 63a). Some sources suggest the *shamir* is the sesame plant, taken up in the story of Ali Baba and the forty thieves, where the phrase 'Open Sesame' gains access to a cave. The fact that the hoopoe can squeeze into the smallest cavities may offer another explanation for the myth.

Several attributes ascribed to the hoopoe are perpetuated in Classical literature, with Aeschylus describing the bird feeding on filth, the overseer of its own evils. In Aristophanes' play *The Birds*, the hoopoe is the king who teaches the other birds to speak and acts as their intermediary, while Ovid's *Metamorphoses* relates the myth of King Tereus of Thrace, who rapes Philomela, the sister of his wife Procne, and cuts out her tongue. In revenge, Procne kills their son and serves him as a stew to his father. On seeing the boy's head presented on a platter, Tereus grabs a sword but just as he attempts to kill the sisters, all three are transformed into birds: Procne a swallow, Philomela a nightingale, and Tereus a hoopoe. The bird's crest indicates his royal status, with his long, sharp beak a symbol of his violent nature.

The bird's objectionable smell led to the Romans dubbing the hoopoe the patron saint of manuring, and narratives in Christian culture maintained its fouling reputation for a long

❖ Artist unknown, *Solomon Receives a Message from the Hoopoe* (detail), second half of the seventeenth century, drawing with use of gouache and gold on paper.

Habiballah of Sava, 'The Concourse of the Birds', *c.* 1600, Folio 11r from a *Mantiq al-Tayr* (Language of the Birds) by Farid al-Din, ink, opaque watercolour, gold and silver on paper.

Artist unknown, *Birds and Fowers*, Edo period, eighteenth century, part of a six-panel screen, ink and colour on silk.

time. Thankfully, pseudo-scientific lore of the bird nesting in debris, detailed in medieval bestiaries, gave way by the Renaissance to realistic depictions of the hoopoe's splendour, made under careful observation and devoid of moral significance, as seen for instance in the beautiful watercolour by Pisanello.

A legendary folktale from Manipur in India tells of two royal brothers, Yoimongba and Taothingmang, who come up with a plan to clean the rivers and streams of the Manipur valley. All the birds participate except Nongoubi, the 'crow pheasant', under the command of his hoopoe master, Chongaraba. As a penalty for his negligence, the brothers forbid Nongoubi from drinking water from the rivers or lakes.

In classical Chinese poetry, the hoopoe is identified as a heavenly messenger and considered an auspicious bird. It was known as the 'mountain monk', conjuring images of a contemplative, solitary figure perched on high vantage points, lost in meditation. Its prominent crest, reminiscent of a monk's cowl, has been interpreted as a sign of wisdom and spiritual enlightenment, and the bird is linked accordingly with scholarship and intellectual pursuits. It appears frequently in Chinese art as a harbinger of good fortune, prosperity and longevity. Thanks to its colourful appearance, especially the vibrant crest, the bird has been linked to rainbows and sunshine and is often seen as a symbol of joy and positive energy. Some legends suggest that encountering it is a sign of divine favour and protection.

COAST & SHORELINE

Standing soldier-erect with spectacled eyes, festively coloured parrot-like beak and orange-red splayed feet, the unmistakable Atlantic puffin (*Fratercula arctica*) commands immediate affection. A bird of the sea, it breeds on North Atlantic coasts and islands, wintering as far south as the Mediterranean and North Carolina.

The folklore of the puffin is long and mysterious. The Irish considered it a sacred bird, believing that the reincarnated souls of Celtic monks dwelt within them, and in the Faroe Islands they are known as *prestur* or priests, reflecting the bird's distinctive colouring and solemn demeanour, in particular its slow walk with head bowed and pontificating call. In Iceland, puffins were thought to predict stormy weather, flying on to land two to three days before a gale. King Arthur was said to appear in his favourite haunts in Wales and Cornwall in the guise of a puffin, chough or raven, and so it was deemed unlucky to kill any of these birds.

The mystery and confusion surrounding the puffin increased during the Middle Ages, with Muslim and Jewish scholars unable to determine whether various birds including puffins and geese were fish, decreeing that they should not be eaten as their origin was unknown. The view was compounded in the Catholic Church, with cardinals identifying such birds as fish rather than flesh. However, salting young birds allowed them to be classified as 'bird-fish', sufficiently satisfying ecclesiastical consciences to mean the birds could be eaten during Lent.

Puffins and other auks feature in Native American mythology. As they endure stormy winter weather at sea, many coastal communities regarded them as weather forecasters, and they were said by the Inuit to have the power to change weather patterns and fend off storms. For religious purposes, the Inuit donned regalia often consisting of

John James Audubon, '*Fratercula arctica*' (Common or Arctic Puffin), no. 93, pl. 464, 1844, from *The Birds of America*, vol. VII.

Jennifer Angaiak Wood, *Inuit Mask of a Puffin*, 2019, alder wood, acrylic paint and feathers.

the skins, crests and beaks of the Atlantic puffin and its relatives the horned puffin (*Fratercula corniculata*) and crested puffin (*Fratercula cirrhata*). Northwest Coast tribes formed puffin clans and carved the birds' images on totem poles, and some Inuit tribes would collect puffin bills to create a musical instrument called 'a shaker', which was held to have magical powers to heal the sick. An Inuit mask from Cape Romanzof, Alaska, was carved from a single piece of wood to represent the bird's spirit or soul.

Archaeological excavations of caves and other habitations along the coasts of Britain and Scandinavia reveal that puffins were farmed for meat and feathers as far back as the last ice age, some 10,000 years ago. Remains at a Romano-British site at Nornour on the Isles of Scilly suggest that the oil of puffins and other seabirds was taken to be used in lamps. Their dense, water-resistant skins must have also provided warm clothing.

Although by most accounts the flavour of puffin meat was disagreeable, it was much sought after by coastal communities and eaten fresh, salted in brine, braised, boiled, stuffed or smoked and dried. The bird's eggs were also collected and eaten, though not to the same extent as those of other seabirds, being more difficult to extract from their burrows. John James Audubon, whose paintings show he was clearly enamoured with the puffin's behaviour, was not impressed with its palatability. Nevertheless, the meat was widely deployed in North America for baiting lobster pots and puffin feathers were used in bedding.

One of the earliest depictions of the puffin in art is an engraving by William Faithorne, published in Francis Willughby's *Ornithology* of 1678. It is a brave attempt, given the strictures of the time, but has little resemblance to the bird's posture and unique appearance. John James Audubon drew puffins from specimens lent to him by the English ornithologist John Gould. His painting displays two adults in breeding plumage: one head-on and foreshortened in its burrow, the other positioned on guard and in profile to show off its rainbow-coloured beak. Charles Tunnicliffe's compositions made in the 1950s capture the character of the puffin, along with its habitat. The pink thrift, white sea campion and colour and formation of the rock face suggest the painting was done on Skomer Island off the southwest coast of Wales, a noted colony for puffins and other seabirds.

✣ Lucian Freud, *Rotted Puffin*, 1944, Conté and coloured crayon on paper.

✳ John Bellany, *Spes Maris*, early 1980s, oil on canvas.

✣

The puffin continues to inspire affection and amusement in adults and children alike. Lundy Island, north of the Devon coast, issued its own coins and stamps with denominations in 'puffins' in 1929, and the Faroe Islands followed suit sometime later. In 1939 Penguin Books introduced a range of titles for children under the Puffin brand, and many readers took up the cause of bird conservation. The French eco charity Agir pour la Biodiversité (Act for Biodiversity) uses a pair of Atlantic puffins as its emblem.

SPES MARIS
Bellany

*

Over northern lakes, the distinctive, haunting calls of the common loon (*Gavia immer*) – known in the UK as the great northern diver – have enchanted or troubled humans for centuries. The bird embodies the spirit of wild places and is linked in many cultures with the beginning and end of life.

A winter visitor to the British Isles, for most of the year the common loon is a widespread resident of lakes and coastal waters in Canada and other northern ranges. For prehistoric people of North America, and later for Native Americans, loons possessed transcendental powers. The Ojibwe (Chippewa) tribe regarded it as the earth-diver, the only animal to successfully dive to the ocean floor to retrieve earth for the creator deity to make land following a great flood. They are also symbols of harmony, generosity and peace for the tribes of the Northwest Coast, used as a clan crest or carved on totem poles. Algonquian tribes of the northeast regard the birds as divine messengers for the creator god, and the Glooscap First Nation, Ojibwa and Menominee possess Loon Clans.

Loons are also believed to wail as they accompany the souls of the dead. Inuit people carried the birds' heads as talismans, and shamanistic practices in Canada and other northern terrains involved imitating the loons' unique cries during ritual performances. Indeed, the role of loons in assisting shamans to see beyond the material world and facilitate passage from one world to the next finds support at excavated Inuit burial grounds in Alaska. Here, human skulls with ivory and jet eyeballs have been discovered next to loon skeletons, and it is likely that the luminous crimson quality of loons' eyes during the breeding season inclined shamans to forge a close relationship with the bird. The eyes of a shaman belonging to the ethnic Yakut population in Siberia were said to have 'a peculiar, unpleasant dull glare, and...their persistent stare...excited and disturbed those upon whom he fixed it'. To this day, individuals destined to become shamans

Artist unknown, sculptured loon, n.d.

John James Audubon, '*Gavia immer*' (Great North Diver, male), no. 96, pl. 476, 1844, from *The Birds of America*, vol. VII.

among the nearby Chukchi people may be recognized first by the quality of their stare.

In Britain, lore and superstitions about the great northern diver largely relate to weather forecasting, going back to ancient beliefs. In Scotland, when loons – including red-throated (*Gavia stellata*, known as the rain goose) and black-throated (*Gavia arctica*) divers – flew inland the weather was likely to be favourable; when flying towards the sea, the opposite was anticipated. The Nlaka'pamux Indians (previously known as the Thompson River Indians) of British Columbia take matters further, believing that the loon could not only foretell rain but in fact cause it, and even a human cry could do the same.

In his *British Zoology* (1766), Thomas Pennant states that the loon (which he calls the immer) was thought to hatch its young in a hole formed by nature under the wing for that purpose. Another 'false' myth was perpetuated in earlier illustrations, when corpses were reassembled in a proud upright posture, which the birds are incapable of achieving.

The necklace of black and white markings around the bird's throat and back became the subject of myth among many Native North Americans. One folktale known across Alaska, northern Canada and Greenland explains how the loon was adorned in return for restoring the sight of a Tsimshian medicine man, who thanked him with his dearest possession,

a necklace of white dentalium shells that caught the loon's neck and scattered the shells across his back. The legend formed the subject of the 1948 Canadian film *The Loon's Necklace*, directed by F. R. Crawley.

Loons also served practical functions. When the Belgian explorer Louis Hennepin was greeted by the Potawatomi of northern Wisconsin in 1679, he was offered a calumet or pipe of peace, noticing as he smoked that: 'They sheath that Reed [the pipe-stem] into the Neck of Birds they call Huars [loons], which are as big as our geese, and spotted with black and white.' In Alaska, the Koyukon people maintain stuffed skins of the loon about their dwellings for decoration, though in earlier times live birds may have been kept for security. Inuit people mostly feed the loon's flesh to dogs, but on the Arctic slopes of Alaska the bird is considered a delicacy. From the Neolithic age until the eighteenth century, the bird was eaten in the islands off Scotland, and its thick layer of fat beneath the skin was used as a cure for sciatica.

The arresting plumage of the male loon has teased many an artist and sculptor to render a worthy portrait, capturing both character and setting. While in Labrador in 1833, John James Audubon drew the common loon in

✻

breeding plumage from a specimen he had just shot. The bird in winter plumage was drawn from a specimen collected some years earlier. Other observers found equal fascination. The nineteenth-century American naturalist and poet Henry David Thoreau chased the loon on Walden Pond in Massachusetts, noting that it cried strangely, 'as if calling on the god of the loons to aid him'. He concluded that 'his god was angry with me, so I left him'.

❈ Richard Kearton, *Black Throated Diver*, 1905, hand-coloured photogravure.

✻ e bond, *Common Loon*, 2021, mixed media.

The great cormorant (*Phalacrocorex carbo*) may be seen along the coasts of Europe, Asia, Africa, Australia and the northeastern regions of North America, flying close to the water with steady wing beats and snake-like neck, or in the distinctive pose it adopts when drying itself, wings outstretched like a cross.

Ill omen or ill served? Literature from Greek and Roman times endowed the cormorant with evil powers and the bird has been persecuted down the ages. The cormorant's blackness aligned it with the crows and sinister stories tell of evil and death. In her classic work *Purity and Danger* (1966), the anthropologist Mary Douglas explored the biblical 'abominations' cited in the books of Leviticus (11:13–19) and Deuteronomy (14:11–20), finding that birds of prey and other eaters of meat, fish and carrion, such as the raven, owl, stork, heron, pelican and cormorant, figure prominently in the lists of dietary prohibitions, the last four also known for their prolific defecation and consequent smell.

The bird's reputation for gluttony, often attempting to swallow a fish larger than its gape, became a frequent foil in literature. Chaucer wrote of the 'hot cormorant of gluttony', while in Shakespeare's *Richard II* (Act 2, scene 1), John of Gaunt evokes the bird to criticize the reckless behaviour of the eponymous king:

With eager feeding food doth choke the feeder;
Light vanity, insatiate cormorant,
Consuming means, soon preys upon itself.

In Victorian times the bird's rapaciousness was likened to that of businessmen, moneylenders, lawyers and clergymen. Corn-dealers were a particular target, prompting puns of corn vorant ('corn devouring') on the bird's name.

Not all associations connected to the cormorant have been negative, however. The symbolic 'liver bird' atop the Liver Building at Pier Head in Liverpool, thought to be a cross between an eagle and a cormorant,

John James Audubon, '*Phalacrocorax carbo*' (Great Cormorant), no. 83, pl. 415, 1871, from *The Birds of America*, vol. VII.

Maker unknown, bird ornament, Maya, 600–800, shell.

has by tradition bestowed good fortune on the maritime city. In the *Odyssey*, Homer related how a sea nymph, transformed into a cormorant, gave Odysseus a magic girdle to save him from death. He also observed the soaking of the birds' feathers and their need to outstretch their wings. The 'wing-drying pose' also features in heraldry and medieval ornamentation, seen as representing the Christian Cross and symbolizing nobility and sacrifice. A quite remarkable painting of a great cormorant appears in the Sherborne Missal (*c.* 1400), displaying the large feet, hooked bill and dark plumage of what is likely a juvenile specimen.

The silence of the double-crested cormorant (*Phalacrocorex auritus*) in flight elicited sympathy in a traditional Native American tale from Haida Gwaii in British Columbia, which tells of how a raven (one of the chief gods) invited a cormorant to go fishing. While the cormorant caught many fish, the raven caught none, so the jealous raven pulled the cormorant's tongue out, leaving it silent. The story is charming, but in reality the bird makes grunting and belching sounds, especially in its breeding colonies.

Humankind has been well served by the cormorant, long exploiting its remarkable fishing skills in a kind of aquatic 'falconry'. Archaeological evidence suggests that cormorant fishing took place in ancient Egypt, Peru, Korea and India, but the strongest tradition has remained in China and Japan, where it is practised commercially. In contrast, it has proved a marginal activity in Britain and much of Europe.

Though cormorants and other seabirds are found in refuse heaps throughout the British Isles dating from the Bronze, Iron and Dark Ages, in later times their numbers remained low in inland waters because fishermen saw them as competitors for fish. Indeed, such was the outcry that Elizabeth I issued an edict listing them as 'noyfull fowls and vermin' and the birds became regularly persecuted. An exception followed when James I and Charles I employed John Wood as Master of the Royal Cormorants for training 'certain fowls called cormorants' and 'making them fit for the use of fishing', along with ospreys and tame otters. Wood 'travelled widely to display the skill of his charges' and recorded the many medicinal benefits of the birds, including 'Dung being hung about the Necks of Infants, [to mitigate] their Cough, and Pain in breeding Teeth'.

In North America, the great cormorant may be a relatively recent arrival from northern Europe, likely following the last glaciation. Refuse heaps on the coastal plain of the southern states have revealed an impressive record of bird consumption involving over fifty species, including cormorants. With the arrival of colonists and later immigrants, hunting and persecution became widespread and is likely

Utagawa Kunisada, *Watching Cormorant Fishing from a Pleasure Boat* (*Ukaibune no asobi*), Edo period, 1852, two of three panels, woodblock print, ink and colour on paper.

⊗ Vittore Carpaccio, *Hunting on the Lagoon* (detail), *c.* 1490–95, oil on panel.

✳ Walter Inglis Anderson, *Dead Cormorant*, 1960–65, watercolour over graphite on off-white wove paper.

to have contributed substantially to population declines in the eighteenth and nineteenth centuries in New England and most of Atlantic Canada. In some parts of northeastern North America, neck feathers were used for decorative wall blankets and primary feathers were formerly in demand for fletching arrows.

Like the smaller double-crested cormorant (*Phalacrocorex auritus*), when a great cormorant flies off from a position above the water, it descends very close to the surface before gathering pace, giving rise to a superstition in the southern United States that 'the shag [an old name for the bird] must wet its tail before it can fly'. A credible likeness appears in Francis Willughby's *Ornithologiae Libri Tres* (1678), especially of the head, but there is little sense of the character of the cormorant. How great a contrast it is with the moving scene of parental care, set on cliffs of Labrador, depicted by John James Audubon, who reported on the bird's massive decline through persecution by fishermen, who saw it as threatening their take.

GREAT CORMORANT *Phalacrocorex carbo*

The common eider (*Somateria mollissima*) is a sturdy, handsome duck that breeds along the northerly coasts of Europe, North America and eastern Siberia, wintering in large flocks in temperate coastal waters. It is the world's most abundant sea duck, exploited by humankind for millennia, especially for its down.

The eider enjoys the reputation of being the fastest bird in level flight, at speeds of 76 km/h (47 mph) as it flies in single file low over the sea, sheltered in troughs between waves. The bird's ability to withstand extremely cold temperatures has made it a symbol of resilience among people of the far north. According to folklore, when small flocks of eiders shelter in Atlantic coves during icy weather conditions, some of the birds move to the outside of the group to prevent the water from freezing. It is also said that non-breeding females known as 'aunts' care for young eider nestlings.

The eggs, meat and down of the common eider have been critical to the subsistence economy of people living on coasts of the northern hemisphere at mid to high latitudes for thousands of years. In Scotland the remains of eider bones have been excavated from caves and refuse heaps dating from Palaeolithic times, and evidence has been found of eider-hunting in Scandinavia from the Neolithic and Bronze Age.

According to legend, the seventh-century missionary and hermit St Cuthbert was said to rear and tame eiders at his home on the island of Inner Farne, off the Northumbrian coast of Britain. Utilizing use of their eggs and down,

William MacGillivray, '*Somatera mollissima*' (Common Eider), pl. 7, 1831–41, from *Watercolour Drawings of British Animals*.

Maker unknown, 'St Cuthbert with Eider Ducks at his Feet', from the East Window at St Cuthbert's Church, Amble, Northumberland, late nineteenth–early twentieth century, stained-glass.

he ensured they were protected, making the island in effect the world's first bird sanctuary. Twelfth-century monks in the nearby city of Durham called eiders 'the birds of the blessed Cuthbert', and to this day they are known locally as Cuthbert's ducks or Cuddy ducks. Although Cuthbert's role was doubtless embellished, many accounts reinforce this special bond between eiders and humans, especially from Icelandic history.

In Native American legends, ducks are invariably gullible, foolish creatures, taken advantage of by trickster animals like foxes or coyotes. Nevertheless, like the common loon, the eider appears in a creation myth in the role of the earth-diver to successfully dive to the ocean floor and bring up earth for the creator deity to make land.

The bird plays a prominent role in the mythology of many Arctic peoples, featuring on wooden masks worn for ceremonial dances and appearing on whistles and carvings in stone, bone or ivory made to honour the duck. A beautiful recent figure shows an eider in a courtship pose, using the colouring of the stone to accentuate its head and wings.

Though revered, the eider has been significantly hunted by northern indigenous cultures for its down, shot from boats using arrows, bird darts, harpoon throwers or multi-pronged spears. The Chukchi people of Arctic Siberia used a hunting weapon called a bola, made from small ivory balls attached to lines of braided sinew tied together at one end, to catch eider when flocks flew overhead during migration. Inuit communities would use the down from as many as twenty-two birds to line dog or sealskin parkas for warmth. The fascinating documentary *People of a Feather*, made in 2011, examines the historical relationship between the Sanikiluaq community of Hudson Bay and the eider.

It is highly probable that the eider was one of the species sought by colonial feather hunters on Canada's Labrador coast in the eighteenth century. Records show that before 1750 vessels were fitted out in New England to collect feathers and eiderdown. Landing on coasts

and islands when the young birds were still unfledged and their moulting parents unable to fly, their crews corralled and clubbed the birds to death, destroying 'millions' of them for their feathers alone (apparently there was no market for their meat). This continued for a decade, until the numbers of birds were so reduced that the practice became unprofitable. In the early twentieth century, the noted American ornithologist Edward Howe Forbush lamented that 'ever since, eggers, fishermen, and settlers have destroyed both birds and eggs. Eider nurseries along the Labrador coast are little more than a memory, and now we import eider-down gathered by the wiser and more humane people of the Old World.'

The few 'portraits' of the eider made prior to the eighteenth century are far from convincing,

but later there was a rush to exploit the bird's image in a frozen setting. In his *Illustrations of British Ornithology* (1819–34), Prideaux John Selby includes a common eider shown swimming in a choppy sea, while John James Audubon depicts an intruding male seen off by two mated 'sea ducks', as they were known in Labrador.

Bruno Liljefors, *Common Eiders on Rocky Islets*, 1897, oil on canvas.

WETLANDS

The mandarin duck (*Aix galericulata*) has held a special place in Eastern cultures for centuries as a symbol of love, fidelity and partnership. The male is an arresting bird, sporting a beautiful pattern of iridescent red, brown, orange and green and a 'sail' of feathers over its back during the breeding season. For its striking appearance, it has been called a 'punk duck'.

Closely related to the equally attractive North American wood duck (*Aix sponsa*), the mandarin duck is native to much of Eurasia, with large introductions of the species to the British Isles and western Europe and smaller introductions in North America. The plumage of the male and female birds differs significantly, with the colouring of the female much more subdued, and in China their name (*yuanyang*) is used informally in Cantonese to refer to an unlikely pair or 'odd couple'.

The fact that the male and female mandarin duck are frequently spotted together in the wild and recognized for their long-term relationships (though in fact the bird itself only remains faithful through the breeding season) has made the birds a popular subject in art and literature, especially in China, from where their reputation spread to Japan, Korea and Vietnam. A pair of mandarin ducks is a frequent motif in Asian vases, fabrics, screens and sculptures, often paired with a lotus plant to represent serenity.

Before the association with romantic love in China, mandarin ducks were used to symbolize a brotherly bond, with an anonymous poem of farewell from one brother to another lamenting: 'We two were trees linked limb to limb, you and I were like one body; we were once those ducks that mate for life, now split like the stars'. They were first linked to romance during the Tang dynasty (618–907 CE), when the poet Lu Zhaolin wrote in *Changan Guyi* of how lovers 'envy the happiness of a pair of mandarin ducks rather than the immortals'. The lines grew so famous that the relationship between mandarin ducks and an inseparable couple in love became ingrained in the Chinese consciousness.

The origin of the mandarin duck as a symbol of eternal love can perhaps be traced to a

Chinese folktale in which Yuan Ge, a gardener, forms a romance with Ying Mei, the daughter of an official, Hong Fu, whose garden he had been hired to tend. On hearing Ying Mei's cries for help from a lotus pond, Yuan Ge jumps in to save her, but her father interprets his actions as an effort to take advantage of his daughter and promptly imprisons him. Visiting Yuan Ge's prison cell in secret one night, Ying Mei gives him a multicoloured robe. The guards report the visit to her father, who tells them to bind stones to Yuan Ge's feet and throw him in the pond. Ying Mei, distressed and devastated, dives into the water behind him. A few days later two beautiful mandarin ducks are swimming on the pond. The vibrant colour of the male was just like the robe Ying Mei had gifted to Yuan Ge, and so people thought the couple had been transformed into birds.

In Feng Shui mandarin ducks are placed in pairs at the centre of a dining room, living

Lü Ji, *Mandarin Ducks and Cotton Rose Hibiscus* (detail), late fifteenth century, hanging scroll, ink and colour on silk.

George Edwards, '*Aix galericulata*' (Mandarin Duck), 1743, from *A Natural History of Uncommon Birds*.

room or bedroom as a way for married couples to settle conflicts, improve bonds and attain marital bliss, or for single individuals to attract their ideal mate. If someone in a loving relationship is keen to marry, a red ribbon or piece of string is tied around the ducks' necks as a symbol of marriage. The connection with marriage extends to Korea, where mandarin ducks represent peace, fidelity and plentiful offspring, with carved wooden pairs often given as wedding gifts. Similarly, in Japan, the birds (*oshidori*) appear in the phrase *oshidori fūfu* or 'a couple of lovebirds' for a happily married couple.

Mandarin ducks frequently appear in Chinese art to symbolize conjugal affection and fidelity. In Ren Yi's *Mandarin Ducks and Lotus*, the aquatic lotus floating on the water signifies purity and rebirth in Buddhist belief, while above them a pair of swimming mandarin ducks suggest the intimacy associated with lifelong partnership. A similarly intimate scene is rendered by the Japanese master Matsumura Keibu, in which a pair of mandarin ducks swim together beneath a snow-laden, red-berried nandina plant, again as a symbol of conjugal fidelity.

In Europe, the mandarin duck was first described and illustrated in 1727 by the German explorer Engelbert Kaempfer, who wrote in his *History of Japan* about

One kind particularly I cannot forbear mentioning, because of the surprizing beauty of its male, call'd Kinmodsui, which is so great, that being shew'd its picture in colours, I could hardly believe my own Eyes, till I saw the Bird it self, it being a very common one.

✤ Yōshū (Hashimoto) Chikanobu, *Chiyoda Castle* (Album of Women) (detail), 1895, triptych of woodblock prints.

✻ Utagawa Kuniyoshi, *Kawazu Saburô Sukeyasu as the spirit of the mandarin duck and Matano Gorô with lantern, scene from a kabuki play*, 1845–47, woodcut.

Later, the English naturalist George Edwards included an illustration and a description of the species under the name 'Chinese teal' in the second volume of his *Natural History of Uncommon Birds* (1743). His hand-coloured etching was based on a live specimen kept by the merchant Matthew Decker on his estate at Richmond in Surrey.

Once widespread in East Asia, large-scale exports of the mandarin duck, along with the destruction of its forest habitat have reduced populations in eastern Russia and China to below 1,000 pairs. Japan is believed to hold some 5,000 pairs, and perhaps 7,000 now live in Great Britain, having escaped from collections.

Waiting in perfect stillness at the water's edge, the breeze caressing its colourful plumage, the heron stands poised to strike its prey. In flight it is quiet and ponderous, as if carried along by the wind that buffets its watery habitat, and its elegant form has beguiled onlookers across continents and centuries.

With a sinuous neck and fearsome harpoon-like beak, the great blue heron (*Ardea herodias*) appears across most of North and Central America, along with the Caribbean and the Galapagos Islands. Its counterpart on the other side of the Atlantic is the very similar grey heron (*Ardea cinerea*), native throughout temperate Europe and Asia, which differs only by its smaller size, greyer, paler neck and the absence of the great blue's rufous thighs.

In ancient Egypt, the grey heron played a role in the world's creation in the form of Bennu, the earthly manifestation of the primal creator god Atum and the sun god Ra, represented in hieroglyphic form as a heron. The bird came to symbolize the cycle of life and death, with the sun rising anew each morning. It was also linked to the god Osiris, who represented the underworld, resurrection, and the cycle of fertility marked by the flooding of the Nile. In the Egyptian Book of the Dead, many scenes associate the heron with the mythical phoenix, while in more prosaic contexts during the Fourth Dynasty it was frequently portrayed near fowlers, indicating that it was domesticated for use as a decoy when trapping wildfowl with nets.

Maker unknown, relief fragment with two birds in the papyrus thicket, Middle Kingdom, *c.* 1925–1900 BCE, limestone and paint.

Frans Snyders, *Fable of Fox and Heron*, 1630s, oil on canvas.

In Classical times, herons often served as a portent or omen. In the *Iliad*, Athena sends a heron to encourage Odysseus and Diomedes on a night mission to infiltrate the enemy camp, the bird calling out in the darkness to comfort them. Ovid's *Metamorphoses* describes a heron emerging for the first time from the smoking ruins of the town of Ardea, in the south of Rome, after it was ransacked by the Trojan hero Aeneas: 'a tall, pale bird that shook the town's grey ashes from its wings and uttered a mournful cry'. For Roman prophets the heron was a bird of divination, which heralds a coming event with its call, while to the Roman poet Lucan it was an omen of bad weather: 'I do not like these signs...the heron dares to fly aloft, trusting his storm-tossed feathers' (*Pharsalia*, V, 551–56).

The portentous qualities associated with the heron are echoed in other cultures too. In Chinese paintings the grey heron symbolizes a path or way (when shown with a lotus, a sense of progression is added). For the Japanese, it is valued as a divine creature, able to ward off misfortune; in a popular animated fantasy film *The Boy and the Heron* (2023), a boy befriends a talking heron after the death of his mother, the bird representing spirits and connections to other worlds.

In Native American folklore, the heron is admired for its fishing skills and good judgment, held up as a symbol of curiosity, purpose and the independence to make wise decisions. If Northwest Coast Native American fishermen spot a heron, it signals a promising fishing trip. The Hitchiti admired the bird's determination and guile, recounted in the story of the heron and the hummingbird, while Algonquian legends led some tribes to consider it a war bird, with its wing and tail feathers worn by warriors reaching a particular status. For many tribes the heron remains a symbol of 'going with the flow',

❈ John James Audubon, '*Ardea herodias*' (Great Blue Heron, Male), no. 74, pl. 369, 1843, from *The Birds of America*, vol. VI.

✳ Jan Weenix, *Gamepiece with a Dead Heron*, 1695, oil on canvas.

of working with Mother Nature's elements rather than struggling against her. However, the bird is also associated with vanity and a weakness for flattery and on occasion is depicted as a restless loner, reflecting its solitary lifestyle.

In some Celtic lore, the grey heron was associated with the gods and portrayed as a peaceful bird. Later in Christianity it was imbued with good luck and a long life, and features in hymns that sing of its patience and stillness in waiting. For a long time, a folk belief in Britain held that herons were thought to possess a special ability to attract fish, with its foot exuding a scent that lured them within reach. The famous angler Izaak Walton supported this view in his *Compleat Angler* (1653), stating that 'some affirm, that any bait anointed with the marrow of the thigh-bone of a heron, is a great temptation to any fish', a claim quashed by Frank Lowe in 1954. Other explanations for the heron's success in fishing include the belief that its powder down feathers are luminous, allowing it to fish by night; that swirling hairs on the bird's legs entice fish; or that they wriggle their toes under the water to simulate worms. In southern Ireland, it was held that small eels pass uninjured through the intestines of a heron, so that it swallows the same individual several times.

Curiously, a combination of a wish to protect fisheries and the heron's desirability as a source of food led to the birds becoming a choice target for falconers; and because they flew high and tried to avoid conflict rather than fight, they gained a reputation for cowardice. This was exploited by the exiled nobleman Robert III of Artois, who presented the English king Edward III with a dish of roasted herons – cowardly birds for a cowardly king who refused to invade France.

The bird is rarely depicted in early manuscripts, but a well-coloured grey heron or 'heyron' does appear in the Sherborne Missal, standing on both feet grasping marginal decoration; a second is rendered less well but adopts the characteristic one-legged pose while swallowing an eel. Louis Nicolas – the first writer to describe all wildlife in North America in his *Histoire Naturelle des Indes Occidentales* – included a pen-and-ink sketch in his *Codex Canadensis* (*c.* 1700) of the great blue, accompanied by an owl and crane. In Britain, Thomas Bewick was among the first to draw the grey heron, shown in profile grappling with an eel, describing a bird 'of a melancholy deportment and fixed to the spot like a stump of a tree'. John James Audubon chose to portray the great blue both in its common form and in a white morph known as the great white heron (*Ardea occidentalis*), thought to be a separate species at the time.

Artist unknown, *Gray Heron (Aosagi) and Mizu-aoi Plant*, 1857, woodblock print.

青鶖
アヲサギ
水葱
甲十六ウ

Of the twenty different species of stork, it is the white stork (*Ciconia ciconia*) that has best captured legend, celebrated as a bringer of babies, a loyal carer for elderly parents and a harbinger of spring. An early appearance in Greek myth of a stork carrying a baby in its beak has endured to this day.

In ancient Egypt, storks were renowned for their piety towards their ageing parents and were occasionally mummified. Both the Egyptian and the Greco-Roman worlds believed that storks demonstrated loyalty by returning to the same nest every year and caring for their parents in old age. This was reflected in an ancient Greek law called Pelargonia (from *pelargos*, meaning stork), requiring citizens to take care of their elderly parents, and a similar Roman law, the *lex ciconiaria* or *antipelargia*. More generally, the stork was seen as a symbol of piety, natural gratitude and fidelity, because it was thought that storks punished infidelity and distained marital betrayal among humans. Jews also held affection for the bird, with the Hebrew word *chasidah* for white stork meaning 'merciful' or 'kind'.

In the third century CE the Roman writer Aelian noted in *De natura animalium* that when storks have nothing to feed their young, they will disgorge their own food and offer it to their offspring. Such positive associations with piety continued into the Christian tradition, where the stork is seen to attack snakes in the fight against the devil, represented in the form of a serpent. In numismatic art the stork appears alongside the figure of Pietus, hands uplifted in prayer. *The Concert in the Egg* (1475–80), attributed to the Dutch artist Hieronymus Bosch, is an allegorical oil painting that plays on the trope of the ship of fools to present a collection of foolish or sinful characters; a white stork stands in the background, perhaps as a symbol of birth or purification.

An early linking of the stork with babies appears in a Greek myth that tells of how the jealous goddess Hera turned a rival queen into a stork, which in turn tried to steal Hera's son. The association with new life can also be traced to the timing of the stork's migration, with the Romans noting the arrival of the white stork in spring, alerting farmers to plant their vines. In Petronius' *Satyricon*, the former slave Trimalchio calls the stork a beloved foreign guest, exiled during winter and

Jan Christiaan Sepp, *The White Stork*, 1739–1811, hand-coloured etching and engraving.

After Hieronymus Bosch, *The Concert in the Egg* (detail), c. 1561, oil on canvas.

a token of warm weather to come. The bird was similarly revered by Muslims because it made an annual pilgrimage to Mecca at the time of its migration.

During the medieval period in Europe, couples would hold their weddings during the summer solstice, believing that it favoured fertility, and nine months later the return of the stork was hoped to herald the arrival of a child. The association spread across the continent in folklore, especially in eastern Europe, and could have been considered useful in answering children's questions about where babies came from.

The taboo nature of this subject was especially strong in the nineteenth century, when Hans Christian Andersen popularized the legend of the stork. In his fairy tale, sleeping babies are brought to families by storks, who pick them up at ponds and lakes. Birthmarks on the back of a newborn baby's head are sometimes referred to as 'stork bites'. In an astounding parallel, in North America the role as 'baby deliverer' was also popular in Sioux legend, though attached to the native wood stork (*Mycteria americana*) rather than the white stork. The association remains a familiar motif in popular culture, for instance with Mr Stork delivering the baby elephant to his mother in the animated Disney film *Dumbo* (1941).

Not all folklore connected with storks was positive. A Polish tale relates how God made the stork's plumage white, but the devil gave it black wings, imbuing it with both good and evil. In Germany the bird was linked to stillborn or disabled babies, thought to have been dropped by the stork en route to the household or as punishment for past wrongdoing. Geoffrey Chaucer's view of the stork as the 'avenger of adultery' persisted in medieval England, possibly inspired by its elaborate courtship posture.

According to Aristotle, when injured in a fight storks (along with other birds) heal their wounds with origanum, a genus of herbaceous perennial flowering plants. Pliny takes this further, writing that a stork's stomach was believed to be a powerful remedy against all poisons (especially with the addition of sheep's milk) and that eating stork chicks was considered a remedy for conjunctivitis.

Interest in the white stork initiated an early understanding of bird migration, as some were found in Europe with African arrows embedded in their bodies, demonstrating that birds migrate rather than hibernating or changing form in winter. A well-known example, discovered in the summer of 1822, was mounted as a taxidermy specimen complete with the ornate African arrow in place.

❉ Artist unknown, *Rama and Lakshmana Search in Vain for Sita*, *c.* 1680–90, ink and opaque watercolour on paper.

✻ Karl Muhlmeister, 'Stork', 1900, from *A Cheerful Picture Book with Old and New Rhymes* by Hans Lustig.

MUTE SWAN

SPECIES Cygnus olor

Native to Europe and western Asia, the graceful mute swan (*Cygnus olor*) is one of the largest birds capable of flight. Often associated with romance and loyalty, they mate for life and are known to grieve a lost partner or cygnet. Nevertheless, the bird also has a darker side as a formidable fighter.

In ancient Greece the swan was held up as a symbol of love and beauty, for instance in the famous myth of Leda and the swan. In the tale, king of the gods Zeus longs to make love to Leda, wife of the king of Sparta. Having been repeatedly rebuffed, he transforms himself into a swan and seduces her. Leda went on to lay two eggs, from which hatched the famously beautiful Helen of Troy and her brother Polydeuces. The opportunities for salacious depictions offered by the myth made it a popular subject in Western painting from the Renaissance onwards, explored by artists from Leonardo da Vinci to Paul Cézanne.

As well as celebrating the bird's beauty, the Greeks believed the swan's long curving neck to be ideal for producing a variety of sounds; indeed, the word 'swan' itself derives from the Indo-European root *swen*, meaning to sound or sign. This gave rise to the famous expression 'swan song', for a final gesture or performance given before retirement or death. The legend of the swan song is used by Aesop in his fable of the Swan and the Goose, in which the swan's song saves its life when it is caught by mistake instead of a goose. In Aeschylus' play *Agamemnon*, Clytemnestra compares the dead Cassandra to a swan who has 'sung her last lament', while in Plato's *Phaedo*, Socrates admonishes his friends for protesting his imminent death: 'And you seem to think I am inferior in prophetic power to the swans who sing at other times also, but when they feel that they are about to die.' The idea was reinforced by Aristotle, who states in his *History of Animals* that swans 'are musical and sing chiefly at the approach of death', and by the third century BCE the belief had become a proverb. Perpetuated

further by the Romans, the myth of the swan song continued to influence Western culture, referenced by Chaucer in his *Parlement of Foules* and by Shakespeare in *The Merchant of Venice.*

Though appearing in different mythologies across the world, there is little consistency in the symbolism attached to the mute swan and tales alternate between celebration of its beauty and fear of its destructiveness. In some regions the bird embodies feminine attributes, but more often it is a masculine symbol inspiring bravery and strength, noting that in the breeding season the swan can turn violent when its offspring is threatened. In a departure from traditional narratives, Hans Christian Andersen's fable

John Gould, '*Cygnus olor*' (Mute Swan), 1862–73, from *The Birds of Great Britain.*

Paul Cézanne, *Leda and the Swan*, *c.* 1880, oil on canvas.

After Leonardo da Vinci, *Leda and the Swan*, before 1517, tempera on panel.

Larry Colwell, *New York City Ballet, Swan Lake*, 1944–66, photographic print.

of the Ugly Duckling tells of a cygnet who is ostracized by his fellow fowls for his homeliness, but grows up to be a beautiful swan, exposing the deceptive nature of first appearances and teaching that true beauty grows from within.

Celtic, Gaelic, Siberian and Chinese myths tell of maidens turning into swans after death. In Norse mythology two swans drank from the sacred well in the home of the gods, the water proving so pure that everything that touched it turned white, including the original pair of swans and their descendants. The warrior goddesses the Valkyries possessed the power to transform into swans. In Hinduism the swan (typically the mute) is a vehicle for many deities, and people who attain great spiritual capabilities are called 'Great Swans' for their ability to travel between various spiritual realms.

As well as artists, the swan's beauty and mythology have inspired composers, for instance Tchaikovsky's famous ballet *Swan Lake*, Jean Sibelius's composition *The Swan of Tuonela*, influenced by epic Finnish tales of the underworld, and Richard Wagner's operas *Lohengrin* and *Parsifal*.

In Britain since the twelfth century, the monarch retains the right to ownership of all unmarked mute swans in open water, though King Charles III exercises the privilege only on certain stretches of the Thames and its surrounding tributaries. The ownership is shared with the ancient livery companies of the Vintners and the Dyers. In the moat of the Bishop's Palace at Wells Cathedral, mute swans have for centuries been trained to ring bells via strings to beg for food, and two swans are still able to ring for lunch today.

*

Jan Asselijn, *The Threatened Swan*, *c.* 1650, oil on canvas.

With their distinctive shape, call in flight and balletic mating behaviour, cranes have been variously held to carry joyful or ominous significance since ancient times, with the earliest depictions appearing on pillars dating to around 9500 BCE at the Neolithic site of Göbekli Tepe in southeastern Turkey.

Found on every continent except Antarctica and South America, all fifteen species of crane have long legs and necks, and most sport greyish or white plumage marked with black and red facial patches. Some species migrate, while others do not.

The common crane (*Grus grus*) was often represented in processions on the walls of ancient Egyptian tombs and temples, with bearers shown bringing the birds as food offerings. It was believed that cranes transported smaller birds on their backs because they could fly such great distances unmatched by other birds.

In ancient Greece the crane was often seen as an omen. According to one myth, the sixth-century BCE lyric poet Ibycus was attacked by thieves, and as he lay dying called to a flock of passing cranes for vengeance. The cranes followed the attackers and hovered over them until, stricken with guilt, the thieves confessed to the robbery and killing. In another, Gerana, queen of the Pygmy folk on the Nile, refused to worship the goddess Hera and was turned into a crane. In the *Iliad* the trumpeting of cranes during migration is invoked to recall the roar of the Greeks at Troy. Depictions of battles between cranes and dwarf people, known as geranomachy, are a widespread motif in antiquity, also seen in China and the Middle East.

Elsewhere in Greek and Roman mythology, dancing cranes are a symbol of joy and a celebration of life, associating the bird with Apollo, the god of prophecy. Both cultures observed the behaviour and flight patterns of the crane to predict the weather or decipher the future, and its migration south was used as a sign for farmers to plough in late autumn. Pliny wrote that cranes would appoint a sentry to stand guard while they slept, holding a stone in its claw; if it fell asleep, it would drop the stone to wake it up. The association with vigilance carried through into Christianity, with the seventh-century bishop and author Isidore of Seville writing that cranes (*grues*) take their name 'from the murmuring sound they make and ever vigilant in taking turns acting as guards'. The image of a crane holding a stone remains a widespread symbol of vigilance, particularly in heraldry.

The crane is held in particular esteem in China and Japan, symbolizing happiness, eternal youth and immortality, and representing one of the five Confucian relationships, the deference

⊗ Gerald of Wales, cranes taking it in turns to sleep, late twelfth to early thirteenth century, from *Topographia Hibernica*, illuminated manuscript.

✳ John James Audubon, '*Grus americana*' (Whooping Crane, Male, adult), no. 63, pl. 313, 1842, from *The Birds of America*, vol. v.

❈ Maker unknown, *Woman's Haori with White and Red Cranes*, 1920–40, silk.

✻ Utagawa Hiroshige, 'Minowa, Kanasugi, Mikawashima', 1856–58, from the series *One Hundred Famous Views of Edo*, woodblock print.

名所江戸百景

of the son to the father. In some traditions it is said to carry the souls of the dead to heaven, while the fluidity and grace of the crane's movements in the wild inspired many styles of kung fu. For the Japanese in particular, cranes also symbolized good luck and longevity, due to their fabled lifespan of a thousand years.

The bird is an established emblem in Chinese painting: two cranes flying towards the sun signify ambition; a crane among clouds represents nobility; a pair together mark a wish for a long-married life, with one crane in pine trees a wish for a long life together. A seventeenth-century Japanese scroll, almost 14 metres (46 ft) in length, by the artist Tawaraya Sōtatsu and calligrapher Hon'ami Kōetsu, depicts a spectacular flock of 100 cranes rendered in gold and silver clay. In simple brushstrokes, the beauty and energy of the birds' soaring posture are regarded as unparalleled.

The courtship dance of the crane, accompanied by a loud trumpeting call, has made the bird highly significant and revered in the art, music and literature of South Asia. The legendary Sanskrit poet Valmiki penned the first *shloka* couplet (*c.* 400–200 BCE) after seeing a male sarus crane (*Antigone antigone*) killed by an arrow while dancing with its mate. In Hinduism it is considered a sacred bird, associated with devotion and marital harmony, and some texts forbid the eating of its meat.

The crane is also held sacred to many First Nation peoples, who often use its feathers in spiritual ceremonies. The Chippewa depicted it in pictographs and rock drawings to symbolize wisdom and communication, while in the Ojibwe language the crane is called the 'echo-maker', reminding one to think carefully before speaking and to express oneself clearly and honestly.

The blue crane (*Grus paradisea*) is the national bird of South Africa, highly regarded for its bravery and hunting ability and claimed to help bring peace to the land. Zulu chiefs wear blue crane feathers in their headdresses as a sign of honour. Uganda's coat of arms, flag and currency bear the image of the grey crowned crane (*Balearica regulorum*) to represent the country's nationhood and unity.

The crane continues to be seen as a symbol of peace, hope and healing today. In the Peace Park in Hiroshima, Japan, thousands of paper cranes can be seen suspended on strings and, currently, the demilitarized zone between North and South Korea serves as a sanctuary for the red crowned crane (*Grus japonensis*). The love of the bird shared by many Koreans is sometimes seen as a symbol that one day the two divided countries will unite once more.

Tawaraya Sōtatsu, *Anthology with Crane Design* (detail), seventeenth century, ink and colour on paper.

Artist unknown, *Krishna Vanquishing the Crane-Demon Bakasura*, late 1700s, gum tempera and gold on paper.

The spectacle of an osprey (*Pandion haliaetus*) diving into water like a meteor and rising up again clasping a thrashing fish in its mighty talons has captivated humans throughout the ages. Today, its arrival in northern climes is a harbinger of spring enjoyed on every continent except Antarctica.

Also known as the fish hawk or sea hawk, the osprey's diet is almost exclusively fish. To help it in hunting for food, it has unique behaviours and specialized characteristics that have been a source of both fascination and suspicion. Pliny reported that adult birds made their young fly up to the sun as a test, dispatching any that failed, while so impressive were its fishing skills that in medieval times people believed that fish simply turned belly-up in surrender to the bird, recorded in George Peele's play *The Battle of Alcazar*, first published in 1594 (Act 1, scene 1):

I will provide thee of a princely osprey,
That as she flieth over fish in pools,
The fish shall turn their glistening bellies up,
And thou shalt take thy liberal choice of all.

Later, in *Coriolanus* (Act 4, scene 7), Shakespeare made reference to fishes' instinctive fear of the bird: 'I think he'll be to Rome / As is the

Neil Welliver, *Osprey's Nest*, 1979, colour woodcut on gampi paper.

John Gould, '*Pandion haliaetus*' (Osprey), 1862, from *The Birds of Great Britain*, vol. 1.

osprey to the fish, who takes it / By sovereignty of nature.' The medieval priest and historian Gerald of Wales stated that the osprey's two feet had different purposes and structures, one designed for catching fish and the other webbed for swimming. In heraldry, the osprey – called a 'sea eagle' – is typically depicted as a white eagle, often with a fish in its talons or beak.

In twelfth-century Ireland, it was thought that the flying osprey excreted a fatty substance to attract fish, and that its oily plumage had a similar effect when immersed in water. Variations on this kind of belief are found in several cultures in subsequent centuries, with the sixteenth-century naturalist William Turner noting that 'fishermen...anoint their bait with osprey's fat, thinking thereby to make them the more efficacious'. The story was recorded in North America in preacher George Henry Loskiel's *History of the Moravian Mission among the North American Indians* (1794), though whether the belief was genuinely held by Native Americans or imported is difficult to determine. Either way, the oil or fat of the osprey was clearly judged by Native Americans to hold curative powers. The Cherokee mixed the substance with old bear oil and drank the concoction as a cure for tuberculosis; a bird's right wing was burned, powdered and steeped in water, to be consumed for the same purpose.

As well as being admired, the osprey's extraordinary fishing abilities have sometimes led to the bird being considered a nuisance, and an abundance in sixteenth-century Britain caused Turner to note that 'the osprey is a bird much better known to-day to Englishmen than many whom keep fish in stews would wish: for within a short time it bears off every fish'. Unsurprisingly it suffered persecution from landowners wishing to protect their stocks of fish and was threatened by collectors of its eggs and skin. The osprey became extinct as a breeding bird in England and Wales in 1847, Ireland in 1875 and in Scotland in 1916, with the poet W. B. Yeats summoning the grey wandering osprey as a manifestation of sorrow in his epic poem *The Wanderings of Oisin* (1889). Today, the bird's tenacity provides much encouragement, and it is not surprising that it has become a popular and powerful totem for conservationists.

Native American peoples generally held the osprey in greater respect, regarding it as a type of eagle. For some, it played 'policing' roles, and spotting one was considered a portent of peril.

As the 'fish hawk', the Nez Perce tribe deemed it to be a medicine bird, and seeing one in a vision or dream was a sign of having been granted spiritual powers as a healer. In the nineteenth century, Arthur Elwood Wright, a 'river Indian' of the Nanticoke tribe of Chesapeake Bay and Delaware, claimed that an osprey's nest found in a spruce pine contained a lodestone that had a magnetic ability to bring the bird back to the same nest each spring (it is now long established that ospreys frequent the same nest year after year). The lodestone was also said to repel lightning.

The osprey has been historically viewed in a positive light in East Asia. In Japanese art and folklore, it is held up as an emblem of endurance, perseverance and the ability to overcome adversity, with its fishing skills admired as a symbol of resourcefulness. The well-known ancient Chinese poem *Guan ju*, thought to date from the seventh century BCE, begins with the line '*Guan guan*, trill the ospreys on the islet in the river'. The bird's onomatopoeic cry of *guan guan* means to join or bring together, with the bird considered a symbol of fidelity and harmony between a husband and wife, owing to its monogamous nature.

Perhaps the earliest accurate depiction of an osprey in colonial North America is found in Mark Catesby's *Natural History of Carolina, Florida and the Bahama Islands* (1731–43), where his 'fishing hawk' (labelled 'Accipiter piscatorius') is shown with a fish grasped in its claws, in a profile somewhat suggestive of a taxidermized specimen. In his later depiction, John James Audubon positions the fish facing forward, to aerodynamically reduce wind

❋ Japanese school, *Osprey*, nineteenth century, woodblock print on paper.

✻ Edwin Austin Abbey, *Figure Study (woman with osprey headdress and white fur colour)*, *c.* 1871–1911, oil on canvas.

resistance. The placement of the bird's powerful wings creates the illusion that they are beating, and both bird and fish are gasping for air. But it is perhaps the contemporary Canadian artist Robert Bateman who best captures the moment when the osprey breaks the water's surface in pursuit of its prey.

With its remarkable resilience and resolve in the face of adversity, in recent times the osprey has come to represent positive responses to nature and is featured on more than fifty international postage stamps. In 1994, it was officially adopted as the provincial bird of Nova Scotia in Canada.

Whether swirling in a flock over the lakes of the Great Rift Valley in Africa or foraging as individuals along a wetland, the exotic appearance and eccentric behaviour of the flamingo has struck humans across the world perhaps like no other bird.

There are six species in total, four in the Americas and the Caribbean and two in Afro-Asia, all of them a distinctive red or shocking pink colour, with very long necks and legs and oddly shaped bills. In recognition of their colour, the English name flamingo derives from the Latin word *flamma*, meaning flame. The bird's unique appearance has often led it to be portrayed as an almost fantastical creature: who can forget the croquet game in Lewis Carroll's *Alice's Adventures in Wonderland* (1865), in which 'the balls were live hedgehogs, the mallets live flamingoes'?

Such fabled associations go back to ancient times, and speculation is rife that the flamingo may have inspired the myth of the phoenix, given its red plumage and identification with flames. Reports of these 'fire birds' from eastern Africa reached the Greeks, and in the *Annals* the historian Tacitus gives a full if sceptical account of their features (book 6, ch. 28); acknowledging that 'All this is full of doubt and legendary exaggeration', he nevertheless concludes that 'there is no question that the bird is occasionally seen in Egypt'.

Some of the earliest artistic representations of flamingos are preserved on decorated ceramic vessels from Pre-Dynastic Egypt, where well-defined flocks (sometimes as many as twenty birds) are shown as a silhouetted line on a wavy design suggestive of a wetland habitat. A faithful later depiction of the bird represents the ornamental hieroglyph for red on a fragment from the tomb of Rahotep at Meidum.

During the reign of Emperor Augustus (r. 27 BCE–14 CE) and later, flamingos were taken to Rome from Egypt and North Africa for their flesh and tongues to be eaten at feasts with an abundance of spices and sauces. As well as for food, flamingos were used as lovers' gifts and exhibited in wealthy Roman villages as live animals. They feature on mosaic decorations found in the southern Mediterranean dating from the first to seventh centuries CE where, despite the apparent familiarity, the repetition of small errors such as the lack of webbed feet betrays poor scientific knowledge of the bird. Flamingos also appear on many early

Sir John Tenniel, *Alice trying to play croquet with flamingo and hedgehog*, 1866, pencil drawing.

Leopold Joseph Fitzinger, *'Phoenicopterus roseus'* (Greater Flamingo), 1864, from *Bilder-atlas zur Wissenschaftlich-populären Naturgeschichte der Vögel in ihren sämmtlichen Hauptformen.*

❖ Raphaël Delorme, *Flamante Rose*, n.d., oil on canvas.

✱ Alexander Calder, *Flamingo*, 1973, sheet metal and paint.

Christian mosaics, accompanied by lush vegetation and other exotic creatures, to extol the beauty of paradise; among the most notable examples are the mosaic floors of a palace in Caesarea Maritima on the Mediterranean coast of Israel.

The Moche people in ancient Peru often depicted the Andean flamingo (*Phoenicoparrus andinus*) on their pottery vessels. According to traditional stories, the flamingo was a saviour of animals because of the way it can bend its neck and its exceptional abilities on land and in flight; some legends even said the birds were men in flamingo form. Miners working in the Andes have been known to kill flamingos for their fat, believing it to cure tuberculosis. In pre-Columbian Mexico the sacred Quecholli bird, whose bright red feathers were used to adorn arrows and javelins in rituals celebrating the hunting season, may well have been the American flamingo (*Phoenicopterus ruber*).

The English colonial artist John White made a remarkable watercolour of an American flamingo on his voyages through the West Indies and along the Florida coast in 1583–93, recording the bird's unique anatomy and soft pink plumage. Following White's portrait, in his own *Natural History of Carolina, Florida and the Bahamas* (1731–43), Mark Catesby noted that 'The figure of each beak is truly hyperbolical' and the black teeth 'an admirable invention of nature; by the help of which...this bird holds his slippery prey the faster'. But it was Audubon who captured the essence of the flamingo's startling colour and demeanour on seeing a flock of them when sailing from the small island of Indian Key, off the coast of Florida, in May 1832.

*

A wading bird found in much of Africa and some parts of Iraq, Iran and Kuwait, the African sacred ibis (*Threskiornis aethiopicus*) played its most significant symbolic role in ancient Egypt, where it was venerated as a manifestation of Thoth, the god of wisdom and learning, thought to help maintain order in the universe.

Portrayed with the head of an ibis on the body of a man (or sometimes a baboon), Thoth played an important role in Egyptian creation myths. In one story, he was a self-created deity who in the form of an ibis laid the cosmic egg that birthed the whole universe. This was thought to have taken place at Hermopolis, and the site became the chief sanctuary of the deity, with numerous public ceremonies and festivals held at the temple in his honour.

Pilgrims came from all over Egypt to bring offerings of ibises to Hermopolis and other temples to be sacrificed, and at the peak thousands of ibises were mummified each year and buried in giant catacombs. The Greek historian Herodotus claimed that dozens of breeding facilities (which he calls *ibiotropheia*) were established to sustain the growing demand, each producing around 1,000 birds annually for mummification (though DNA studies suggest that wild birds provided the bulk of the supply).

It is estimated that between 330 BCE and 390 CE eight million ibises were mummified and entombed in Thoth's honour, especially at the necropolises of Tuma el-Gebel and Saqqara. The birds were often young and usually killed by breaking the neck. For mummification the head and bill were often placed between the tail feathers, and a piece of food such as a snail was placed in the bird's bill for the afterlife. Different burials were given according to whether the bird was a pet or an offering, and some sacred birds were afforded a special type of mummification, transported to temples and honoured with a more luxurious burial. During the time of the pharaohs, wild ibises were protected by law. In the late eighteenth century Napoleon Bonaparte's army brought mummified specimens of the sacred ibis back to Europe, and French naturalists used them

Maker unknown, inlay depicting Thoth as the ibis with a maat feather, Late Period–Ptolemaic Period, fourth century BCE, faience.

Robert Jacob Gordon, '*Threskiornis aethiopicus*' (Holy Ibis), 1778, pen and ink, watercolour.

to demonstrate a lack of evolution, noting that there were very few differences between 3,000-year-old specimens and their living counterparts. By the 1850s the species had become extinct in Egypt, perhaps as a result of habitat loss.

Herodotus and Pliny report that the ibis was invoked against incursions of winged serpents, and Pliny records that flies which brought pestilence would die immediately if an ibis was sacrificed to the gods. It has been suggested that the 'winged serpents' and 'flies' refer to locusts. Other Roman authors assert that crocodiles and snakes are rendered harmless on being touched by an ibis feather. Later, the Roman-Jewish historian Josephus states that when Moses led the Hebrews to wage war on the Egyptians, he brought with him numerous caged ibises to repel serpents.

As well as Thoth, the ibis became associated with the Egyptian goddess Isis, whose worship spread to ancient Rome, especially among women, and the bird appears in Roman frescoes and mosaics, including one discovered at Pompeii. Right up to the nineteenth century and beyond, artists continued to incorporate ibises into their works to evoke the 'East'; in a painting of a young woman by the French Impressionist Edgar Degas, for instance, along with an Eastern-looking cityscape in the background, two ibises lend an air of unfamiliarity and exoticism to a largely Western audience.

Leon Jean Joseph Dubois, 'Thoth twice great, presiding over the lower region', 1823–25, from *Egyptian Pantheon: a collection of mythological figures from ancient Egypt, based on monuments, with explanatory text.*

Edgar Degas, *Young Woman with Ibis*, 1857–58, reworked 1860–62, oil on canvas.

ENVOI

From the south they come,
The birds, the warlike birds,
With sounding wings.
I wish to change myself
To the body of that swift bird.
I throw my body in the strife.

'From the South' (Chippewa)

As we have seen throughout this book, birds hold a universal place in the human experience. Since the earliest times, diverse peoples around the world have endowed them with myths, omens and magical powers, and woven them as symbols into their cultural and social histories. Unlike some other animals, birds are often near at hand, yet for many their soaring flight provided a link between the heavens and the earth. For sedentary peoples, their migrations signalled the changing seasons and a time to plant or reap. Observing the flight pattern of seabirds also helped anticipate changing weather conditions and navigation on the high seas.

In many cultures, birds were regarded as messengers, carrying tidings or warnings from loved ones and the spirit world, reporting deaths and injuries and channelling divine intelligence to answer questions. Gods with sacred powers appeared in the form of birds, communicating important messages via auguries to shamans, priests and prophets during trances or other mystical states. Jewish, Christian and Islamic traditions portrayed angels with bird wings and devils with bat wings, assuming much the same role as prophetic birds in Greek and Roman traditions as messengers between God (or the gods) and human beings. In Asia, bird mythology inclines towards associations with love, fidelity and happiness, compassion, watchfulness and good fortune: the magpie is seen as sinister in Europe and North America but regarded as a bringer of good fortune in Asia. In Australasia, birds often represent protection, renewal or wisdom.

Across the world, mythologies and legends often bear a striking similarity, despite the peoples who tell them perhaps never or rarely having had contact with each other. The earth-diver creation myth of many North American peoples, for

Samuel Jessurun de Mesquita, *Egret*, 1913, print.

Michelino da Besozzo (attr.), *Madonna of the Rose Garden*, 1420–35, tempera on panel.

example, also exists in northern Europe and northeastern Asia, suggesting that Native American versions may have originated in ancient myths shared with distant Asian ancestors.

If birds provided simpler and more interpretative signs to explain mysterious events or deaths, linking them to supernatural causes frequently produced superstitions that resulted in birds suffering opprobrium and persecution, as witnessed especially with ravens, owls and accipiters. As animism (a belief that nature has a soul) and superstitions ceded to religious practices, spiritual connections to birds and other wildlife have been progressively eroded, if not lost. In parallel, the natural environment has been subjugated to a technological world that increasingly separates humans from significant connection or interaction with nature.

Depending on the season, I am fortunate to have many of the birds included in this book within sight of my North American home: common loons, great-crested cormorants, great blue herons, barn swallows, winter wrens, cedar waxwings, ravens, house sparrows, American goldfinches. They provide constant delight and, in writing this book, have helped me understand their connection with the myths and legends of ancient and modern cultures.

The author Margaret Atwood has argued that 'myths lay out pretty clearly what's on the human smorgasbord: what we want, what we fear, what we would like to have, what we would very much not like to have...Those human fears and human desires really have not changed, and they're reflected in the myths that have been with us for a long time.'[1] Myth depicts the truths of human nature: who we are as people, how we behave and why, and animals, especially birds, are fundamental to our seeking answers to these questions and helping us to understand, in the words of Jonathan Bate, 'the relationship between nature and culture [as] the key intellectual problem of the twenty-first century'.[2]

❖ Melchior d'Hondecoeter, *The Floating Feather*, c. 1680, oil on canvas.

1 Margaret Atwood, interviewed by Bill Moyers for the television series *Bill Moyers on Faith & Reason*, 28 July 2006.

2 Jonathan Bate, 'Foreword', in Laurence Coupe (ed.), *The Green Studies Reader: From Romanticism to Ecocriticism*, London and New York, 2000.

I would like to thank Ben Hayes and India Jackson of Thames & Hudson for their great help in bringing the book to fruition, and Felicity Maunder for her editorial oversight. Thanks also to the wider team, Maria Ranauro for her work on the images, Aman Phull for the beautiful design and Ginny Liggitt for the production work.
As always, thanks to my wife Valerie and my son Ian for their encouragement and support.

SELECTED BIBLIOGRAPHY

Adair, James, *The History of the American Indians* (1775), ed. Kathryn E. Holland Braund, Tuscaloosa, AL, 2004

Addison, Josephine, *Treasury of Bird Lore*, London, 1998

Allen, Paula Gunn, *Song of the Turtle: American Indian Literature, 1974–1994*, New York, 1996

Armitage, Simon, and Tim Dee (eds), *The Poetry of Birds*, London, 2009

Armstrong, Edward Allworthy, *The Folklore of Birds: An Enquiry into the Origin & Distribution of Some Magico-Religious Traditions*, London, 1958

—— *The Life and Lore of the Bird in Nature, Art, Myth, and Literature*, New York, 1975

Anker, Jean, *Bird Books and Bird Art: An Outline of the Literary History and Iconography of Descriptive Ornithology*, Copenhagen, (1938) 1990

Anderson, Peter, '"Thickening, deepening, blackening": Starlings and the Object of Poetry in Coleridge and Dante', *The Coleridge Bulletin*, new series 32 (2008), pp. 55–62

Arnott, W. Geoffrey, *Birds in the Ancient World from A to Z*, New York, 2007

Attenborough, David, and Errol Fuller, *Drawn from Paradise: The Discovery, Art and Natural History of the Birds of Paradise*, London, 2012

Atwood, Margaret, interviewed by Bill Moyers for the television series *Bill Moyers on Faith & Reason*, 28 July 2006

Audubon, John James, *Ornithological Biography; or an Account of the Habits of the Birds of the United States of America*, Philadelphia, 1831–39

—— *The Birds of America*, Edinburgh and London, 1827–38

Avery, Mark, *Remarkable Birds*, London and New York, 2016

Backhouse, Janet, *Medieval Birds in the Sherborne Missal*, Toronto, 2001

Bailleul-LeSuer, Rozenn (ed.), *Between Heaven and Earth: Birds in Ancient Egypt*, Chicago, 2012

Bate, Jonathan, 'Foreword', in Laurence Coupe (ed.), *The Green Studies Reader: From Romanticism to Ecocriticism*, London and New York, 2000

Beike, Marcus, 'The History of Cormorant Fishing in Europe', *Vogelwelt*, vol. 133 (2012), pp. 1–21

Bergen, Fanny D. (ed.), *Animal and Plant Lore: Collected from the Oral Tradition of English Speaking Folk*, Boston and New York, 1899

Berglund, Axel-Ivar, *Zulu Thought-Patterns and Symbolism*, London, 1976

Birkhead, Tim, *Birds and Us: A 12,000-Year History, from Cave Art to Conservation*, London, 2022

—— *The Magpies: The Ecology and Behaviour of Black-billed and Yellow-billed Magpies*, London, 1991

—— *The Wisdom of Birds: An Illustrated History of Ornithology*, London, 2008

Boag, David, and Mike Alexander, *The Puffin*, London, 1995

Boas, Franz, 'Mythology and Folk-Tales of the North American Indians', *The Journal of American Folklore*, vol. 27, no. 106 (1914), pp. 374–410

Bonnefoy, Yves (ed.), *Asian Mythologies*, Chicago, 1993

Bugler, Caroline, *The Bird in Art*, London, 1997

Catesby, Mark, *The Natural History of Carolina, Florida, and the Bahama Islands, Containing the Figures of Birds, Beasts, Fishes, Serpents, Insects and Plants*, 2 vols + Appendix, London, 1731–43 (Appendix 1748)

Choskyi, V. J., 'Symbolism of Animals in Buddhism', *Buddhist Himalaya*, vol. 1, no. 1 (1988), pp. 1–5

Clark, Kenneth, *Animals and Men: Their Relationship as Reflected in Western Art from Prehistory to the Present Day*, New York, 1977

Clark, R. T. Rundle, *Myth and Symbol in Ancient Egypt*, London and New York, 1959

Cocker, Mark, with photographs by David Tipling, *Birds and People*, London, 2013

Cohen, Simona, *Animals as Disguised Symbols in Renaissance Art*, Leiden, 2008

Corera, Gordon, *Operation Columba, The Secret Pigeon Service: The Untold Story of World War II Resistance in Europe*, New York, 2018

Czaplicka, M. A., *Aboriginal Siberia: A Study in Social Anthropology*, Oxford, 1914

Damas, David, and William C. Sturtevant (eds), *Handbook of North American Indians: Volume 5 – Arctic*, Washington, DC, 1985

Darlington, Miriam, *Owl Sense*, London, 2018

David, Arlette, 'Hoopoes and Acacias: Decoding an Ancient Egyptian Funerary Scene', *Journal of Near Eastern Studies*, vol. 73, no. 2 (October 2014), pp. 235–52

De Kay, Charles, *Bird Gods*, New York, 1898

Eastman, John, *Birds of Field and Shore*, Mechanicsburg, PA, 2000

Edmonds, Michael, *Taking Flight: A History of Birds and People in the Heart of America*, Madison, WI, 2018

Elphick, Jonathan, *Birds: The Art of Ornithology*, London, 2008

Eriksson, Paul S., *Treasury of North American Birdlore*, ed. Alan Pistorius, Middlebury, VT, 1994

Ferris, Iain, *Cave Canem: Animals and Roman Society*, Stroud, 2018

Fisher, Celia, *The Magic of Birds*, London, 2014

Fisher, James, *Birds as Animals, 1: A History of Birds*, London, 1954

Fitzpatrick, J., 'Folklore of Birds and Beasts of India', *Journal of the Bombay Natural History Society*, vol. 28, no. 2 (1923), pp. 562–65

Flores, Dan, *Wild New World: The Epic Story of Animals and People in America*, New York, 2022

Forbush, Edward Howe, *A History of the Game Birds, Wild Fowl and Shore Birds of Massachusetts and Adjacent States*, Boston, 1916

Forrester, Ron, and Ian Andrews (eds), *The Birds of Scotland*, 2 vols, Aberlady, 2007

Fowke, Edith, *Folktales of French Canada*, Toronto, 1979

French, John, *The Art of Distillation, Book IV: Of Animals*, London, 1651

Friedmann, Herbert, *The Symbolic Goldfinch: Its History and Significance in European Devotional History*, Washington, DC, 1946

Frisby, Helen, '"Them Owls Know": Portending Death in Later Nineteenth- and Early Twentieth-century England', *Folklore*, vol. 126, no. 2 (2015), pp. 196–214

'The Golden Peacock', Jewish Folk Songs, https://www.jewishfolksongs.com/en/golden-peacock (accessed August 2025)

Green, Miranda J., *Dictionary of Celtic Myth and Legend*, London and New York, 1992

Grove Day, A., *The Sky Clears: Poetry of the American Indians*, Lincoln, NE, 1951

Gurney, John Henry, *Early Annals of Ornithology*, London, 1921

Guy, John, and Deborah Swallow (eds), *Arts of India, 1550–1900*, London, 1990

Hadler, Mona, 'Manet's "Woman with a Parrot" of 1866', *Metropolitan Museum Journal* (1973), www.journals.uchicago.edu/doi/10.2307/1512646 (accessed August 2025)

Hamilton, Virginia, *The People Could Fly: American Black Folktales*, New York, 1985

Hancock, James, and Hugh Elliott, *The Herons of the World*, New York, 1978
Harrison, Colin, *The History of the Birds of Britain*, London, 1988 Houlihan, Patrick F., with Steven M. Goodman, *The Birds of Ancient Egypt*, Cairo, 1988
Hyland, Angus, and Caroline Roberts, *The Book of the Raven: Corvids in Art and Legend*, London, 2021
Idema, Wilt L., transl. and intr., *Personal Salvation and Filial Piety: Two Precious Scroll Narratives of Guanyin and Her Acolytes*, Honolulu, 2008
Ingersoll, Ernest, *Birds in Legend, Fable and Folklore*, New York, 1923
Jackson, Christine E., *Bird Etchings: The Illustrators and Their Books, 1655–1855*, Ithaca, NY, 1985
Johnsgard, Paul A., *Hawks, Eagles, and Falcons of North America*, Washington, DC and London, 1990
Kaempfer, Engelbert, *The History of Japan*, trans. John Gaspar Scheuchzer, 2 vols, London, 1727
Kear, Janet, *Man and Wildfowl*, London, 1990
Keel, Dan, *Swan: Portrait of a Majestic Bird, from Mythical Meanings to the Modern Day*, London, 2022
Kortright, F. H., *The Ducks, Geese & Swans of North America*, Washington, DC, 1943
Krech III, Shepard, *The Ecological Indian: Myth and History*, New York, 1999
—— *Spirits of the Air: Birds and American Indians in the South*, Athens, GA, 2009
Kunstmann, John Gotthold, *The Hoopoe: A Study in European Folklore*, Chicago, 1938
Kushlan, James A., and James A. Hancock, *The Herons*, Oxford, 2005
Lack, Andrew, *Redbreast: The Robin in Life and Literature*, Pulborough, West Sussex, 2008
Larson, Jeanette, and Adrienne Yorinks, *Hummingbirds: Facts and Folklore from the Americas*, Watertown, MA, 2011
Lederer, Roger J., *The Art of the Bird: The History of Ornithological Art through Forty Artists*, Chicago, 2019
Lee, Sam, *The Nightingale: Notes on a Songbird*, London, 2023
Lewis-Stempel, John, *The Secret Life of the Owl*, London, 2017
Lindale, Jean M., *The Natural History of Magpies*, Berkeley, CA, 1937
Lindow, John, *Norse Mythology: A Guide to Gods, Heroes, Rituals and Beliefs*, Oxford, 2001
Lowe, Frank, *The Heron*, London, 1954
Lowther, P. E., et al., 'Atlantic Puffin (Fratercula arctica)', Cornell Lab, Birds of the World, https://birdsoftheworld.org/bow/species/atlpuf (accessed August 2025)
Mails, Thomas E., *The Mystic Warriors of the Plains: The Culture, Arts, Crafts and Religion of the Plains Indians*, New York, 1972
McIntyre, Judith W., *The Common Loon: Spirit of Northern Lakes*, Minneapolis, 1986
Middleton, A. L. A., *American Goldfinch*, Harrisburg, PA, 1989
Mitchell, Jaqueline (ed.), *Birds: An Anthology*, Oxford, 2020
Moss, Stephen, *The Robin: A Biography*, London, 2017
Mynott, Jeremy, *Birds of the Ancient World*, Oxford, 2018
—— *Birdscapes: Birds in Our Imagination and Experience*, Princeton, NJ, 2009
—— *The Story of Nature: A Human History*, New Haven and London, 2024
'Native American Mythology', Encyclopedia.com, www.encyclopedia.com/humanities/news-wires-white-papers-and-books/native-american-mythology (accessed August 2025)
Olson, Roberta J. M., *Audubon as Artist: A New Look at The Birds of America*, London, 2024
Owen, Stephen, *An Anthology of Chinese Literature: Beginnings to 1911*, New York and London, 1996
Pollard, John, *Birds in Greek Life and Myth*, London and New York, 1977
Poole, Alan Forsyth, *Ospreys: A Natural and Unnatural History*, Cambridge, 1989
Price, Alice L., *Swans of the World: In Nature, History, Myth & Art*, Tulsa, 1994
Ratcliffe, Derek, *The Raven: A Natural History in Britain and Ireland*, London, 2011
Rowland, Beryl, *Birds with Human Souls: A Guide to Bird Symbolism*, Knoxville, TN, 1978
Rupp, William J., *Bird Names and Bird Lore Among the Pennsylvania Germans*, Norristown, PA, 1947
Saunders, Nicholas J., *Animal Spirits*, London, 1995
Savage, Candace, *Bird Brains: The Intelligence of Crows, Ravens, Magpies and Jays*, San Francisco, 1995
Sax, Boria, *Avian Illuminations: A Cultural History of Birds*, London, 2021
Seidelman, Harold, and James Turner, *The Inuit Imagination: Arctic Myth and Sculpture*, Vancouver and Toronto, 1993
Selby, Prideaux John, *Illustrations of British Ornithology*, Edinburgh, 1821–34
Shephard, T. V., S. E. G. Lea and N. Hempel de Ibarra, 'The Thieving Magpie? No Evidence for Attraction to Shiny Objects', *Animal Cognition*, vol. 18 (2015), pp. 393–97
Shute, Joe, *A Shadow Above: The Fall and Rise of the Raven*, London, 2018
Swainson, Charles, *The Folk Lore and Provincial Names of British Birds*, London, 1886
Tate, Peter, *Flights of Fancy: Birds in Myth, Legend, and Superstition*, London, 2010
Trevelyan, Marie, *Folk-lore and Folk-stories of Wales*, London, 1909
Tyler, Hamilton A., *Pueblo Birds & Myths*, Flagstaff, AZ, 1991
Uglow, Jenny, *Nature's Engraver: A Life of Thomas Bewick*, London, 2006
Vaughan, Richard, *In Search of Arctic Birds*, London, 1992
Vesey-Fitzgerald, Brian, *British Game*, London, 1946
Walton, Izaak, *The Compleat Angler: or, The Contemplative Man's Recreation* (1653), 6th edn, London, 1793
Warren-Chadd, Rachel, and Marianne Taylor, *Bird: Myth, Lore and Legend*, London, 2016
Watson, Jeff, *The Golden Eagle*, Princeton, NJ, 1997
Welch, Patricia B., *Chinese Art: A Guide to Motifs and Visual Imagery*, Tokyo, 2008
Welker, Robert Henry, *Birds and Men: American Birds in Science, Art, Literature, and Conservation, 1800–1900*, Cambridge, MA, 1955
Wellesley, Mary, *The Gilded Page: The Secret Lives of Medieval Manuscripts*, New York, 2020
Werness, Hope B., *The Continuum Encyclopedia of Animal Symbolism in World Art*, London and New York, 2007
Weslager, C. A., *The Nanticoke Indians: Past and Present* (1948), Newark, DE, 1983
Yapp, Brunsdon, *Birds in Medieval Manuscripts*, London, 1981
Zimmerman, Larry J., *The Sacred Wisdom of the American Indians*, London, 1999

SOURCES OF ILLUSTRATIONS

Dimensions are given in centimetres followed by inches, height precedes width precedes depth, unless otherwise stated.

a = above; **b** = below; **l** = left; **r** = right

Images in the Bird Index are all details taken from images reproduced elsewhere in the book.

Front endpapers

Mughal school, *Bee-eater*, nineteenth century, from the Kevorkian album, opaque watercolour and gold on paper, 16.9 × 10.9 (6 ¾ × 4 ⅜). Freer Gallery of Art Collection, Purchase – Charles Lang Freer Endowment. National Museum of Asian Art, Smithsonian Institute, Washington, DC (F1948.21a)

Carel Fabritius, *The Goldfinch* (detail), 1654, oil on panel, 33.5 × 22.8 (13 ¼ × 9). Mauritshuis, The Hague (605)

After Leonardo da Vinci, *Leda and the Swan*, before 1517, tempera on panel, 115 × 86 (45 ⅜ × 33 ⅞). Galleria Borghese, Rome (434)

Back endpapers

Jacques Barraband, '*Diphyllodes magnificus*' (Magnificent Bird-of-Paradise), from *Histoire naturelle des oiseaux de paradis et des rolliers, suivie de celle des toucans et des barbus* by François La Vaillant, Paris, 1806. Rare Book Division, The New York Public Library (b14444167)

John James Audubon, '*Pelecanus occidentalis*' (Brown Pelican, Adult Male), no. 85, pl. 423, from *The Birds of America*, vol. VII, New York, 1844. General Research Division, The New York Public Library (b13559627)

Jacques Barraband, '*Paradisaea rubra*' (Red Bird-of-Paradise), from *Histoire naturelle des oiseaux de paradis et des rolliers, suivie de celle des toucans et des barbus* by François La Vaillant, Paris, 1806. Rare Book Division, The New York Public Library (b14444167)

1
Edouard Manet, *Young Lady in 1866* (detail), 1866, oil on canvas, 185.1 × 128.6 (72 ⅞ × 50 ⅝). Metropolitan Museum of Art, New York. Gift of Erwin Davis, 1889 (89.21.3)

2 (181)
Utagawa Kuniyoshi, *Kawazu Saburô Sukeyasu as the spirit of the mandarin duck and Matano Gorô with lantern, scene from a kabuki play* (detail), 1845–47, woodcut, 35.6 × 23.5 (14 × 9 ¼). Metropolitan Museum of Art, New York. Gift of Mary L. Cassilly, 1894 (JP206)

4
Giuseppe Arcimboldo, *Air* (detail), *c.* 1566, oil on canvas, 74.4 × 56 (29 ⅜ × 22 ⅛). Private Collection. Photo Fine Art Images/ Heritage Images/Alamy Photo Stock

6
Frans Snyders, *Concert of Birds*, 1629–30, oil on canvas, 99.2 × 143.5 (39 ⅛ × 56 ½). Museo Nacional del Prado, Madrid (P01758)

7
Maker unknown, Native American (Tsimshian) Raven rattle, nineteenth century, Skidegate, British Columbia, Canada, cedar, pebbles and polychrome, 31 × 10.3 × 10.5 (12 ¼ × 4 ⅛ × 4 ¼). Metropolitan Museum of Art, New York. The Crosby Brown Collection of Musical Instruments, 1889 (89.4.611)

8al, 22
John James Audubon, '*Bombycilla cedrorum*' (Cedar bird or Cedar Wax-wing, 1. Male 2. Female), no. 50, pl. 246, 1842, from *The Birds of America*, vol. IV, New York, 1842. General Research Division, The New York Public Library (b13559627)

8ar, 28
François Nicolas Martinet, '*Carduelis carduelis*' (European Goldfinch), pl. 4, from *Histoire Naturelle des Oiseaux* by Louis-Jean-Marie Daubenton, Paris, 1765. Smithsonian Libraries and Archives

8bl, 34
Leopold Joseph Fitzinger, '*Ectopistes migratorius*' (Passenger Pigeon), from *Bilder-atlas zur Wissenschaftlich Populären Naturgeschichte der Vögel in ihren sämmtlichen Hauptformen*, Vienna, 1864. Smithsonian Libraries and Archives

8br, 38
John Gould, '*Pica caudata*' (Magpie), from *The Birds of Great Britain*, London, 1862–73. Rare Book Division, The New York Public Library (b14484973)

9al, 45
John Gould, '*Erythacus rubecula*' (Robin, or Redbreast), from *The Birds of Great Britain*, London, 1862–73. Rare Book Division, The New York Public Library (b14484973)

9ar, 48
Basil Ede, '*Luscinia megarhynchos*' (Nightingale), pl. 23, from *A Hand-Book to the Birds of Great Britain* by Richard Bowdler Sharpe, vol. I, London, 1894. University of California Libraries

9bl, 57
John James Audubon, '*Tyto alba*' (Barn Owl), no. 7, pl. 34, from *The Birds of America*, vol. I, New York, 1840. General Research Division, The New York Public Library (b13559627)

9br, 53
John James Audubon, '*Troglodytes hiemalis*' (The Winter Wren, 1. Male 2. Female 3. Young), no. 25, pl. 121, from *The Birds of America*, vol. II, New York, 1841. General Research Division, The New York Public Library (b13559627)

10a, 65
John Gould, '*Topaza pella*' (Crimson Topaz Hummingbird), from *A Monograph of the Trochilid, or Family of Humming-birds*, vol. III, London, 1849. Smithsonian Libraries and Archives

10bl, 66
'*Casuarius unappendiculatus*' (One-wattled Cassowary), from *A Monograph of the Genus Casuarius* by Walter Rothschild, Zoological Society of London, 1900. Biodiversity Heritage Library

10br, 70
François-Nicolas Martinet, '*Dacelo novaeguinaea*' (Laughing Kookaburra), pl. 663, from *Planches Enluminées D'histoire Naturelle* by Edme-Louis Daubenton, vol. VII, Paris, 1765–83. Biodiversity Heritage Library

11a, 75
Jacques Barraband, '*Paradisaea minor*' (Small Emerald Bird of Paradise, male), from *Histoire naturelle des oiseaux de paradis et des rolliers, suivie de celle des toucans et des barbus* by François La Vaillant, Paris, 1806. Rare Book Division, The New York Public Library (b14444167)

11b, 72
Leopold Joseph Fitzinger, '*Menura superba*' (Superb Lyrebird), from *Bilder-atlas zur Wissenschaftlich-populären Naturgeschichte der Vögel in ihren sämmtlichen Hauptformen*, Vienna, 1864. Smithsonian Libraries and Archives

12al, 80
Joseph Smit, '*Pavo cristatus*' (Common Peafowl), from *A Monograph of the Phasianidae, or Family of the Pheasants* by Daniel Giraud Elliot, New York, 1872. Rare Book Division, The New York Public Library (b14477911)

12ar, 85
John Gould, '*Trogon resplendens*' (Resplendent Trogon), from *A Monograph of the Trogonodiae, or Family of Trogons*, London, 1835. Smithsonian Libraries and Archives

12c, 88
Leopold Joseph Fitzinger, '*Ara Macao*' (Scarlet Macaw), from *Bilder-atlas zur Wissenschaftlich-populären Naturgeschichte der Vögel in ihren sämmtlichen Hauptformen*, Vienna, 1864. Smithsonian Libraries and Archives

12br, 93
John Gould, '*Ramphastos vitellinus*' (Channel-billed Toucan), from *A Monograph of the Ramphastidae, or Family of Toucans*, London, 1852. Smithsonian Libraries and Archives

13al, 98
John Gould, '*Aquila chrysaetos*' (Golden Eagle), from *The Birds of Great Britain*, vol. I, London, 1862. Rare Book Division, The New York Public Library (b14484973)

13ar, 111
John Gould, '*Falco peregrinus*' (Peregrine Falcon), from *The Birds of Great Britain*, London, 1862–73. Rare Book Division, The New York Public Library (b14484973)

13bl, 106
John James Audubon, '*Corvus corax*' (Raven, Old Male (Thick-Shell bark Hickory)), no. 45, pl. 224, from *The Birds of America*, vol. IV, Philadelphia, 1842. General Research Division, The New York Public Library (b13559627)

13br, 116
Ian Rees, *Andean Condor in Flight*, 2025, colour pencil on Bristol Paper © Ian Rees

14al, 120
Johannes Gerardus Keulemans, '*Apteryx mantelli*' (North-Island Kiwi), from *A History of the Birds of New Zealand* by Walter Lawry Buller, London, 1888. Naturalis Biodiversity Center

14ar, 126
'*Buceros rhinoceros*' (Rhinoceros Hornbill), from *Dictionnaire des Sciences Naturelles*, Paris, 1816–45. Bibliothèque National de France

14c, 123
Archibald Thorburn, *Swift* (detail), *c.* 1915, watercolour and bodycolour over pencil on paper. Bristol Museum and Art Gallery. Photo Iconographic Archive/Alamy Stock Photo

14bl, 130
John James Audubon, '*Hirundo rustica*' (Barn or Chimney Swallow), no. 10, pl. 48, from *The Birds of America*, vol. I, Philadelphia, 1840. General Research Division, The New York Public Library (b13559627)

14br, 136
John Gould, '*Merops apiaster*' (European Bee-eater), from *Birds of Europe*, vol. II, 1837. Smithsonian Libraries and Archives

15al, 139
John Gould, '*Passer domesticus*' (Common or House-Sparrow), from *The Birds of Great Britain*, London, 1873. Rare Book Division, The New York Public Library (b14484973)

15ar, 142
'*Phasianus torquatus*' (Chinese Ring-necked Pheasant), from *Illustrations of Indian Zoology*, by John Edward Gray, London, 1830–34. Rare Book Division, The New York Public Library (b14485023)

15bl, 147
Johannes Gerardus Keulemans, '*Strigops habroptilus*' (Kakapo), from *A History of the Birds of New Zealand* by Walter Lawry Buller, London, 1888. Naturalis Biodiversity Center

15br, 151
John Gould, '*Upupa epops*' (Hoopoe), from *The Birds of Great Britain*, vol. I, London, 1873. Rare Book Division, The New York Public Library (b14484973)

16al, 158
John James Audubon, '*Fratercula arctica*' (Common or Arctic Puffin), no. 93, pl. 464, from *The Birds of America*, vol. VII, Philadelphia, 1844. General Research Division, The New York Public Library (b13559627)

16ar, 163
John James Audubon, '*Gavia immer*' (Great North Diver), no. 96, pl. 476, from *The Birds of America*, vol. VII, Philadelphia, 1844. General Research Division, The New York Public Library (b13559627)

16bl, 166
John James Audubon, '*Phalacrocorax carbo*' (Great Cormorant), no. 83, pl. 415, from *The Birds of America*, vol. VII, Philadelphia, 1871. General Research Division, The New York Public Library (b13559627)

16br, 172
William MacGillivray, '*Somatera mollissima*' (Common Eider), pl. 7, from *Watercolour Drawings of British Animals*, 1831–41. Natural History Museum, London/Alamy Stock Photo

17a, 184
John James Audubon, '*Ardea herodias*' (Great Blue Heron, Male), no. 74, pl. 369, from *The Birds of America*, vol. VI, Philadelphia, 1843. General Research Division, The New York Public Library (b13559627)

17b, 179
George Edwards, '*Aix galericulata*' (Mandarin Duck), from *A Natural History of Uncommon Birds*, London, 1743. National Library Board, Singapore

18al, 188
Jan Christiaan Sepp, *The White Stork*, 1739–1811, hand-coloured etching and engraving. National Gallery of Art, Washington, DC. Gift of Dr. and Mrs. George Benjamin Green (1978.88.2)

18ar, 199
John James Audubon, '*Grus americana*' (Whooping Crane, Male, adult), no. 63, pl. 313, from *The Birds of America*, vol. v. Philadelphia, 1842. General Research Division, The New York Public Library (b13559627)

18b, 192
John Gould, '*Cygnus olor*' (Mute Swan), from *The Birds of Great Britain*, London, 1862–73. Rare Book Division, The New York Public Library (b14484973)

19a, 205
John Gould, '*Pandion haliaetus*' (Osprey), from *The Birds of Great Britain*, vol. I, London, 1862. Rare Book Division, The New York Public Library (b14484973)

19bl, 209
Leopold Joseph Fitzinger, '*Phoenicopterus roseus*' (Greater Flamingo), from *Bilder-atlas zur Wissenschaftlich-populären Naturgeschichte der Vögel in ihren sämmtlichen Hauptformen*, Vienna, 1864. Smithsonian Libraries and Archives

19br, 213
Robert Jacob Gordon, '*Threskiornis aethiopicus*' (Holy Ibis), 1778, pen and ink, watercolour, 36 × 25.2 (14 ¼ × 10). Rijksmuseum, Amsterdam (RP-T-1914-17-321)

20
Hieronymus Bosch, *The Garden of Earthly Delights* (detail), *c.* 1490–1500, triptych, oil on oak panels, 205.5 × 384.9 (81 × 152). Museo Nacional del Prado, Madrid (P002823)

23
Kiyohara Yukinobu, *Waxwings, Cherry Blossoms and Bamboo*, late seventeenth century, hanging scroll, ink and colour on silk, 99.4 × 41.6 (39 ⅛ × 16 ⅜). Metropolitan Museum of Art, New York. Fishbein-Bender Collection, Gift of T. Richard Fishbein and Estelle P. Bender, 2012 (2012.522.2)

24
Robert Greenhalf, *Waxwings*, *c.* 2018, woodcut, 28 × 28 (11 ⅛ × 11 ⅛). © Robert Greenhalf

25l
Lucas Cranach the Elder, *Two Dead Bohemian Waxwings*, *c.* 1530, watercolour on paper, 34.6 × 20.3 (13 ⅝ × 8). Kupferstich-Kabinett, Dresden (C 2179)

25r
Ohara Kōson, *Waxwing on Snow-Covered Branch*, 1900–30, woodcut, 33.1 × 17.9 (13 ⅛ × 7 ⅛). Rijksmuseum, Amsterdam. Gift of J. Perrée, Eindhoven, 1999 (RP-P-1999-450)

26
Raphael, *Madonna of the Goldfinch* (detail), *c.* 1505–6, oil on panel, 107 × 77 (42 ¼ × 30 ⅜). Uffizi, Florence (1447)

27
John Siferwas and others, a 'Grene finch' (misidentified goldfinch), *c.* 1399–1407, from the Sherborne Missal. British Library (Add. 74236, page 364)/Bridgeman Images

29
Hieronymus Bosch, *The Garden of Earthly Delights* (detail), *c.* 1490–1510, triptych, oil on oak panels, 205.5 × 384.9 (81 × 152). Museo Nacional del Prado, Madrid (P002823)

31
Carel Fabritius, *The Goldfinch* (detail), 1654, oil on panel, 33.5 × 22.8 (13 ¼ × 9). Mauritshuis, The Hague (605)

32
John Tarantino, *Crock*, *c.* 1940, watercolour, coloured pencil and graphite on paperboard, 22.8 × 28.4 (9 × 11 ¼). National Gallery of Art, Washington, DC (1943.8.5172)

33
Henri Matisse, *The Birds*, 1947, collage, 20 × 44 (7 ⅞ × 17 ⅜). Private Collection. Photo Bridgeman Images. © 2026 Succession H. Matisse/DACS

35
Torii Kiyoshige, *Minamoto no Yoritomo Hiding in a Tree*, *c.* 1758, colour woodblock print, 31.2 × 44 (12 ⅜ × 17 ⅜). Art Institute of Chicago. Clarence Buckingham Collection (1942.68)

36
Maker unknown, marble grave stele of a little girl, *c.* 450–440 BCE, Parian marble, 80.6 × 37 (31 ¾ × 14 ⅝). Metropolitan Museum of Art, New York. Fletcher Fund, 1927 (27.45)

37
René Magritte, *The Big Family*, 1963, oil on canvas, 100 × 81 (39 ⅜ × 32). Private Collection. Bridgeman Images. © 2026 ADAGP, Paris and DACS, London

39
Félix Bracquemond, *Margot la Critique*, 1854, etching, 23.8 × 20.7 (9 ⅜ × 8 ¼). Metropolitan Museum of Art, New York. Rogers Fund, 1922 (22.15.5)

40
Alessandro Magnasco, *The Tame Magpie* (detail), *c.* 1707–8, oil on canvas, 63.5 × 74.9 (25 × 29 ½). Metropolitan Museum of Art, New York. Purchase, Katherine D. W. Glover Gift, 1984 (1984.191)

41
Francisco de Goya, *Manuel Osorio Manrique de Zuñiga* (detail), 1787–88, oil on canvas, 127 × 101.6 (50 × 40). Metropolitan Museum of Art, New York. The Jules Bache Collection, 1949 (49.7.41)

42
Kees Koeman, *Magpie*, 1910–32, woodcut, 30 × 13.8 (11 ⅞ × 5 ½). Rijksmuseum, Amsterdam (RP-P-1932-928)

43
Joan Miró, Plate (folio 4) from *Il était une petite pie* (Once There Was a Little Magpie), 1928, pochoir, 17.5 × 28 (6 ⅞ × 11). Museum of Modern Art, New York. Gift of James Thrall Soby (49.1958.2). Digital Image The Museum of Modern Art/Licensed by SCALA/Art Resource, NY. © 2026 Successió Miró/ADAGP, Paris and DACS London

44
Sir Joshua Reynolds (circle of), *Babes in the Wood* (detail), *c.* 1770, oil on canvas, 65 × 49.5 (25 ⅝ × 19 ½). Private Collection

46
Cesare Magni (attr.), *Virgin and Child with a Robin* (detail), 1500–49, oil on panel, 39 × 30 (15 ⅜ × 11 ⅞). Musei Civici, Pavia, Italy. Photo Mario Bonotto/Scala, Florence

47
Walter Crane, 'Cock Robin and Jenny Wren', from *The Baby's Opera. A book of old rhymes with new dresses* by Walter Crane, London, n.d., print, 17 × 17 (6 ¾ × 6 ¾). The Miriam and Ira D. Wallach Division of Art, Prints and Photographs: Picture Collection, The New York Public Library

49
Max Ernst, *Two Children Are Threatened by a Nightingale*, 1924, oil on wood with painted wood elements and frame, 69.8 × 57.1 × 11.4 (27 ½ × 22 ½ × 4 ½). Museum of Modern Art, New York (00256.37). © 2026 ADAGP, Paris and DACS, London

50
Paul Klee, *Persische Nachtigallen* (Persian Nightingales), 1917, gouache, watercolour, and pen and black ink over graphite on laid paper, mounted on cardboard, 22.8 × 18.1 (9 × 7 ⅛). National Gallery of Art, Washington, D.C Gift of Catherine Gamble Curran and Family, in Honour of the 50th Anniversary of the National Gallery of Art (1990.59.2)

51
Riza-yi 'Abbasi, *Study of a Bird*, 1634, ink, opaque watercolour, gold and silver on paper, 9.8 × 17.5 (3 ⅞ × 6 ⅞). Metropolitan Museum of Art, New York. Louis E. and Theresa S. Seley Purchase Fund for Islamic Art and Rogers Fund, 1985 (1985.2)

52
Bachiacca (Francesco Ubertini), *Portrait of a Woman with a Book of Music* (detail), c. 1540–45, oil on panel, 103.2 × 80.3 (40 ⅝ × 31 ⅝). J. Paul Getty Museum, Los Angeles (78.PB.227)

54
Charles Fréger, *Wren Boy, Dingle, Ireland*, 2014, from the 'Wilder Mann' series, photographic print. © Charles Fréger

55
Alex Hunt, *Kwakiutl Wren*, twentieth century, red cedar and acrylic paint, 22.9 × 20.3 × 14 (9 ⅛ × 8 × 5 ⅝). Image Courtesy of Waddington's Auctioneers and Appraisers, Toronto

56
Valentine Cameron Prinsep, *The Owl*, 1863, oil on canvas, 77.5 × 54 (30 ⅝ × 21 ⅜). Private Collection

58
Francisco Goya, *Witches*, c. 1797–98, oil on canvas, 45 × 32 (17 ¾ × 12 ⅝). Lazaro Galdiano Museum, Madrid. Photo Prisma Archivo/Alamy Photo Stock

59
Maker unknown, head of a barn owl, 664–150 BCE, limestone and pigment, 108 × 105 × 63 (42 ⅝ × 41 ⅜ × 24 ⅞). Oriental Institute at the University of Chicago (2978)

60
Henri Rousseau, *The Dream* (detail), 1910, oil on canvas, 204.5 × 298.5 (80 ⅝ × 117 ⅝). Museum of Modern Art, New York. Gift of Nelson A. Rockefeller (252.1954). Photo Digital image, The Museum of Modern Art, New York/Scala, Florence

62l
Agostino Aglio, 'Huitzilopochtli', from *Antiquities of Mexico* by Edward King, Viscount Kingsborough, London, 1831. Smithsonian Libraries and Archives

62r
Maker unknown, textile fragment with hummingbirds from India, c. 1750, linen, 85 × 54 (33 ½ × 21 ¼). Rijksmuseum, Amsterdam. On loan from the Koninklijk Oudheidkundig Genootschap (BK-KOG-2609-A)

63
Joseph Constantine Stadler, 'Large flowering sensitive plant', from *New Illustration of the Sexual System of Carolus von Linnaeus* by Robert John Thornton, London, 1807, hand-coloured aquatint, 57 × 48 (22 ½ × 19). The Miriam and Ira D. Wallach Division of Art, Prints and Photographs: Print Collection, The New York Public Library (b13998666)

64
Frida Kahlo, *Self-Portrait with Thorn Necklace and Hummingbird*, 1940, oil on canvas mounted to board, 61.3 × 47 (24 ⅛ × 18 ⅝). Nickolas Muray Collection of Mexican Art. Harry Ransom Center, University of Texas, Austin (66.6)

67
Francis Barlow, *A Cassowary*, c. 1680–90, oil on canvas, 188.6 × 132.7 (74 ⅜ × 52 ¼). Private Collection. Photo Christie's Images/ Bridgeman Images

68l
Jiwaka Tribe from Western Highlands at Mount Hagen Show, Papua New Guinea, head-dresses made from Cassowary feathers, 2011. Photo David Tipling Photo Library/Alamy Stock Photo

68r
Maker unknown, dagger made of Cassowary bone, Papua New Guinea, n.d. Photo David Tipling Photo Library/ Alamy Stock Photo

69
Maker unknown, mask (Buk, Krar or Kara), Torres Strait Islander, mid to late nineteenth century, Mabuiag Island, Australia, turtle shell, wood, cassowary feathers, fibre, resin, shell and paint, 54.6 × 63.5 × 57.8 (21 ½ × 25 × 22 ⅞). Metropolitan Museum of Art, New York. The Michael C. Rockefeller Memorial Collection, Purchase, Nelson A. Rockefeller Gift, 1967 (1978.412.1510)

71
Mick Qulliam, *Kookaburra*, 2017, acrylic on canvas, 81 × 81 (32 × 32). Image courtesy of Art Mob and the artist

73
Damian Cazaly, *The Supurb Lyrebird's Song*, 2018, mural, Rochester, Victoria, Australia. Photo Robert Wyatt/Alamy Stock Photo

74
Paul Klee, *Fairy Tale*, 1929, watercolour on gessoed canvas, 50 × 43 (19 ¾ × 17). Private Collection. Photo Christie's

76
Maker unknown, Rana crown from Nepal, nineteenth century, made with pearls, precious stones and birds-of-paradise feathers. National Museum of Qatar, Doha. Photo Digital Image Library/Alamy Photo Stock

77
Peter Paul Rubens, *Adoration of the Magi* (detail), 1609–28, oil on canvas, 355.5 × 493 (140 × 194 ⅛). Museo Nacional del Prado, Madrid (P01638). Photo MNP/Scala, Florence

78
Artist unknown, *Kakubha-Ragini, a forlorn lady walking amongst peacocks*, *c.* 1775–99, gouache and gold, 27.5 × 18.8 (10 ⅞ × 7 ½). Rijksmuseum, Amsterdam. On loan from the Royal Asian Art Society in The Netherlands, gift of Mr and Mrs Hülsmann-Stork, 1976 (AK-MAK-1261)

79
Enrique Simonet, *The Judgement of Paris* (detail), 1904, oil on canvas, 215 × 331 (84 ¾ × 130 ⅜). Museo de Málaga (BA/DJ02010). Photo Peter van Evert/Alamy Stock Photo

81
Gyorgy Kepes, *Juliet with Peacock Feather*, 1937–38, gelatin silver print with gouache, 15.3 × 11.5 (6 ⅛ × 4 ⅝). Art Institute of Chicago. Maurice D. Galleher Endowment (1996.1). © The Estate of György Kepes (Imre Kepes and Juliet Kepes Stone)

82
Artist unknown (India), *Subramaniyan with his Consorts Valli and Devasena*, *c.* 1900–15, colour lithograph and varnish. 50.5 × 35.2 (19 ⅞ × 13 ⅞). Metropolitan Museum of Art, New York. Purchase, Friends of Asian Art Gifts, 2021 (2021.222)

83
Alexander Calder, *Peacock*, 1941, sheet metal, wire and paint, 93.5 × 126 (36 ¾ × 49 ½). Photo courtesy of Calder Foundation, New York/Art Resource, New York. © 2026 Calder Foundation, New York/DACS, London

84
Diego Muñoz Camargo, 'Battle of Michoacan between the Spanish and the Aztecs', 1892 copy of the sixteenth-century original, illustration from *Lienzo de Tlaxcala*. Photo Archives Charmet/ Bridgeman Images

86
Maker unknown, quetzal feather headdress, sixteenth century, quetzal feathers, gold appliqué and fibre net, 116 × 175 (45 ¾ × 69). Museum für Volkerkunde, Vienna. Photo Bridgeman Images

87
Reproduction of Bonampak Murals, Room 1, from the Mayan temple, Bonampak, Lacandon jungle, Chiapas. Museum of Mexican History, Nuevo Leon, Monterrey, Mexico. Photo Richard Maschmeyer/ Alamy Stock Photo

89
Peter Paul Rubens, *Holy Family with a Parrot*, 1613–15, oil on panel, 164 × 190 (64 ½ × 74.8). Royal Museum of Fine Arts, Antwerp (312)

90
Frida Kahlo, *Me and My Parrots*, 1941, oil on canvas, 82 × 62.8 (32 ⅜ × 24 ¾). Harold H. Stream Collection, New Orleans. Photo Fine Art Images/Bridgeman Images

91
Artist unknown (China), *Guanyin, Bodhisattva of Compassion*, eighteenth century, gold ink on indigo dyed paper, mounted as a hanging scroll, 63.5 × 41 (25 × 16 ⅛). Ruth Chandler Williamson Gallery, Scripps College, Claremont, CA (0322)

92
Raymond Monvoisin, *Dom Pedro II, Emperor of Brazil, at age 21* (detail), 1847, oil on canvas. Pinacoteca do Estado de São Paulo, on loan from a private collection. Photo The Picture Art Collection/Alamy Stock Photo

94
Maker unknown, bird pendant from Costa Rica, 300–700, jadeite, 6.7 × 1.9 × 4.7 (2 ⅝ × ¾ × 1 ⅞). Metropolitan Museum of Art, New York. The Michael C. Rockefeller Memorial Collection, Bequest of Nelson A. Rockefeller, 1979 (1979.206.1138)

95
'Guinness Is Good For You', design by John Gilroy, 1928, modern pub sign, Kilarney, Ireland. Photo Adrian Muttitt/Alamy Stock Photo

96
Harunobu Suzuki, *A young woman kneeling upon the floor of a room, handing a pot with an egg-plant growing in it to a young man with a falcon upon his wrist* (detail), 1891, woodblock print, 27.6 × 20 (10 ⅞ × 7 ⅞). The Miriam and Ira D. Wallach Division of Art, Prints and Photographs: Print Collection, The New York Public Library (113097)

99
Damiano Mazza, *The Rape of Ganymede*, *c.* 1570–90, oil on canvas, 177 × 186.6 (69 ¾ × 73 ½). National Gallery, London (NG1666)

100
Maker unknown, Roman eagle statue, 100–200 CE, bronze, 104.2 × 78.7 × 76.2 (41 × 31 × 30). J. Paul Getty Museum, Los Angeles (72. AB.151)

101
Artist unknown, eagle-headed supernatural being from Nimrud, ninth century BCE, gypseous alabaster relief, 252.1 × 181.61 × 15.24 (99 ¼ × 71 ½ × 6). Los Angeles County Museum of Art (LACMA), Gift of Anna Bing Arnold (66.4.4)

102
Totem poles of the Haida (left) and Kwakwaka'wakw (centre) at Thunderbird Park in Victoria, British Columbia, Canada, 1955, photographic print. Photo Granger/ Bridgeman Images

104
Robert Rauschenberg, *Canyon*, 1959, oil, pencil, paper, metal, photograph, fabric, wood, canvas, buttons, mirror, taxidermied eagle, cardboard, pillow, paint tube and other materials, 207.6 × 177.8 × 61 (81 ¾ × 70 × 24). Museum of Modern Art (MoMA), New York. Gift of the family of Ileana Sonnabend (1782.2012). Digital image, The Museum of Modern Art, New York/Scala, Florence. © 2026 Robert Rauschenberg Foundation/VAGA at ARS, NY and DACS, London

105
Edward S. Curtis, *The Eagle Catcher*, 1908, photographic print. Library of Congress, Washington, DC Prints and Photographs Division (LC-USZ62-96189)

107
Katsushika Hokusai, *The Little Raven with the Minamoto Clan Sword*, *c.* 1823, colour woodcut, 27.5 × 21.7 (10 ⅞ × 8 ⅝). Pushkin Museum, Moscow

108
Chief Charles Edenshaw, *Raven Transformation Mask*, 1880, Haida Gwaii, British Columbia, Canada, cedar wood, feathers, fur, leather, string and nails, 63 × 94 × 38 (24 ⅞ × 37 ⅛ × 15). Photo © Pitt Rivers Museum, University of Oxford (1891.49.8)

109
Paul Gauguin, *Nevermore*, 1897, oil on canvas, 60.5 × 116 (23 ⅞ × 45 ¾). The Courtauld, London. Samuel Courtauld Trust (189065)

110
Mirza 'Ali (attr.), *Princely Hawking Party*, *c.* 1570, ink, opaque watercolour and gold on paper, 47.9 × 20.8 (18 7/8 × 8 3/16). Metropolitan Museum of Art, New York. Rogers Fund, 1912 (12.223.1)

112l
Maker unknown, incised whelk shell cup showing falcon-warrior from Spiro, Oklahoma, *c.* 1100, marine shell, h: 33 (13). Smithsonian Institution, National Museum of the American Indian, Washington, DC. (Cat. no. 125)

112r
Maker unknown, inlay of the Horus falcon on the hieroglyph for 'gold', fourth century BCE, faience, 15.6 × 12.9 (6 1/8 × 5 1/16). Metropolitan Museum of Art, New York. Purchase, Edward S. Harkness Gift, 1926 (26.7.996)

113
Maker unknown, *Hawking Party* (detail), *c.* 1500–30, wool warp and wool wefts, 266.7 × 377.2 (105 × 148 1/2). Metropolitan Museum of Art, New York. Gift of George Blumenthal, 1941 (41.100.195)

114l
Maker unknown, earflare with condor, sixth or seventh century, Peru, Moche, silver, gold, gilded copper and shell, 7.6 × 7.6 × 10.8 (3 × 3 × 4 1/4). Metropolitan Museum of Art, New York. The Michael C. Rockefeller Memorial Collection, Bequest of Nelson A. Rockefeller, 1979 (1979.206.1246)

114r
Maker unknown, vessel with condor and human head, 400–1000, Peru, Tiwanaku style, pottery, 10.4 × 5.5 × 10.5 (4 1/8 × 2 3/16 × 4 1/8). The Cleveland Museum of Art. The Norweb Collection (1949.558)

115
Tumi (knife) with condor, Moche, 200–800, copper, shell, turquoise, 20 × 8.3 × 5.7 (7 7/8 × 3 1/4 × 2 1/4). Metropolitan Museum of Art, New York. Bequest of Jane Costello Goldberg, from the Collection of Arnold I. Goldberg, 1986 (1987.394.217)

117
Nazca lines showing a condor, 200 BCE–500 CE, Peru, geoglyphs made in the soil. Photo © Mary Jelliffe. All rights reserved 2025/Bridgeman Images

118
Vincent van Gogh, *Wheat Field with a Lark* (detail), 1887, oil on canvas, 53.7 × 65.2 (21 1/4 × 25 3/4). Van Gogh Museum, Amsterdam. Photo Album/Alamy Stock Photo

121
Peter Wilson, *Big Hand in the Sky*, 1978, oil on canvas, 213.3 × 152.4 (84 × 60). © Peter Wilson. All rights reserved 2025/ Bridgeman Images

122
Giovanni Bellini (workshop of), *Madonna and Child* (detail), *c.* 1510, oil on wood, 34.3 × 27.6 (13 1/2 × 10 7/8). Metropolitan Museum of Art, New York. The Jules Bache Collection, 1949 (49.7.2)/ Art Resource/Scala, Florence

124
Bruno Liljefors, *Common Swifts*, 1886, oil on canvas, 41 × 56 (16 1/4 × 22 1/8). Stockholms Auktionsverk

125
Vincent van Gogh, *Four Swifts with Landscape Sketches, Paris, April–September 1887*, 1887, pencil, pen, ink and chalk, on paper, 26.9 × 35.2 (10 5/8 × 13 7/8). Van Gogh Museum, Amsterdam (Vincent van Gogh Foundation). Photo Vidimages/Alamy Stock Photo

127
Mansur, 'Great Hornbill' (detail), *c.* 1615–20, folio from the Shah Jahan Album, ink, opaque watercolour and gold on paper, 38.7 × 26.7 (15 1/4 × 10 1/2). Metropolitan Museum of Art, New York. Purchase, Rogers Fund and The Kevorkian Foundation Gift, 1955 (55.121.10.14)

128l
Maker unknown, hornbill-head-shaped throwing knife, n.d., Cameroon, Africa, iron, wood, 28.2 × 26 × 2.8 (11 1/8 × 10 1/4 × 1 1/8). Musée du quai Branly – Jacques Chirac, Paris (71.1948.15.150). Photo musée du quai Branly – Jacques Chirac, Dist. GrandPalaisRmn/image musée du quai Branly – Jacques Chirac

128r
Utagawa Hiroshige, *Purple Magnolia and Hornbill*, *c.* 1830, woodblock print, ink and colour on paper, 37.1 × 12.5 (14 5/8 × 5). Metropolitan Museum of Art, New York. Purchase, Joseph Pulitzer Bequest, 1918 (JP264)

129
Gordon Deacon, *Hornbills*, *c.* 1934, colour relief print, 12.7 × 11.6 (5 × 4 5/8). Published by Works Progress Administration (WPA), Federal Art Project, Philadelphia (1935–1943). Philadelphia Museum of Art. Federal Works Agency, Work Projects Administration, on long-term loan to the Philadelphia Museum of Art from the Fine Arts Collection, U.S. General Services Administration, 1943 (2-1943-276.18)

131l
Artist unknown, room of lilies or spring, Akrotiri fresco, Thera (Santorini), sixteenth century BCE. National Archaeological Museum, Athens, Greece. Photo NPL – DeA Picture Library/Bridgeman Images

131r
Carlo Crivelli, *The Madonna of the Swallow* (detail), *c.* 1490, tempera and gold on wood, 150.5 × 107.3 (41 5/8 × 42 1/4). National Gallery, London (NG724.1). Photo Vidimages/ Alamy Stock Photo

132
Giacomo Balla, *Swallows Flying*, 1913, oil on canvas, 42 × 53 (16 5/8 × 20 7/8). Private Collection, Genoa, Italy. Photo White Images/Scala, Florence. © 2026 DACS

133
Itō Jakuchū, *Swallow and Camellia*, *c.* 1900, woodblock print, 23.5 × 21 (9 1/4 × 8 1/4). Metropolitan Museum of Art, New York. Rogers Fund, 1925 (MJP12)

134–135
Félix Henri Bracquemond, *The Swallows*, *c.* 1881, pen, brush and black ink, with black chalk, graphite and touches of black Conté crayon on tan wove paper, 27.7 × 37.7 (11 × 14 7/8). Art Institute of Chicago. Marjorie Hubachek Watkins Fund in honour of her parents (1998.76)

137
Mughal school, *Bee-eater*, nineteenth century, from the Kevorkian album, opaque watercolour and gold on paper, 16.9 × 10.9 (6 3/4 × 4 3/8). Freer Gallery of Art Collection, Purchase – Charles Lang Freer Endowment. National Museum of Asian Art, Smithsonian Institute, Washington, DC (F1948.21a)

138
Edward Poynter, *Lesbia and her Sparrow* (detail), 1907, oil on canvas, 49 × 37 (19 3/8 × 14 5/8). Private Collection, UK

140a
Maker unknown, Relief with the seer Calchas (sparrow, top right corner), relief 140–160 CE and head 170–190 CE, marble, 145 × 99.5 × 26.6 (57 ⅛ × 39 ¼ × 10 ½). J. Paul Getty Museum, Los Angeles (72.AA.160)

140bl, 140br
John Siferwas and others, marginal decoration, including a male house sparrow and female house sparrow, *c.* 1399–1407, from the Sherborne Missal. British Library (Add. 74236, p.377)/ Bridgeman Images

141
Artist unknown, Garden Fresco from the House of the Golden Bracelet (sparrow top centre), Pompeii, first century CE, water-based pigments on limestone plaster. Museo Archeologico Nazionale, Naples. Photo Album/Alamy Photo Stock

143
Male pheasant in the Lovell Lectionary, southern England (Glastonbury?), *c.* 1400–10. British Library (Harley MS 7026/1 f.5r)/ Bridgeman Images

144
Ring-necked Pheasants Feeding in the Snow, *c.* 1900, Keystone View Co. hand-coloured gelatin silver print. J. Paul Getty Museum, Los Angeles (84.XC.873.7578)

145
John J. Eyers, *Hanging Game Birds (Pheasant)*, 1872, oil on canvas, 66.7 × 48.3 (26 ¼ × 19 ⅛). Philadelphia Museum of Art. Purchased with funds contributed by the Young Friends of the Philadelphia Museum of Art, 2009 (2009-113-1)

148
Maker unknown, *Taiaha kura* (long handled striking weapon) from New Zealand, 1750–1850, wood, feathers, dog hair, pāua (abalone shell), woodcarving, each approx: 175.4 × 6.4 (69 ⅛ × 2 ⅝). Museum of New Zealand Te Papa Tongarewa. Bequest of Kenneth Athol Webster, 1969. Te Papa (WE000273)

149
Maker unknown, the *kahu kākāpō* after conservation and mounting, *c.* 1810s–20s, *whatu kākahu* (cloak weaving) with kakapo feathers, processed flax fibre and European wool, 127 × 109 (50 × 43). Perth Museum (1978.73). Photo © 2022 Trustees of the British Museum/2022 Culture Perth and Kinross

150
Artist unknown, Queen of Sheba and hoopoe, *c.* 1590–1600, ink, opaque watercolour and gold on paper, 10 × 19.5 (4 × 7 ¾). The Trustees of the British Museum (1948,1211,0.8)

153
Artist unknown, *Solomon Receives a Message from the Hoopoe* (detail), second half of the seventeenth century, drawing with use of gouache and gold on paper. Sotheby's

154
Habiballah of Sava, 'The Concourse of the Birds', *c.* 1600, Folio 11r from a *Mantiq al-Tayr* (Language of the Birds) by Farid al-Din, ink, opaque watercolour, gold and silver on paper, 25.4 × 11.4 (10 × 4 ½). Metropolitan Museum of Art, New York. Fletcher Fund, 1963 (63.210.11, f.11r)

155
Artist unknown, *Birds and Fowers*, eighteenth century, part of a six-panel screen, ink and colour on silk, 182 × 369.2 (71 ¾ × 145 ⅜). Freer Gallery of Art Collection. Gift of Charles Lang Freer (F1907.137)

156
Vittore Carpaccio, *Hunting on the Lagoon* (detail), *c.* 1490–95, oil on panel, 75.6 × 63.8 (29 ⅞ × 25 ⅛). J. Paul Getty Museum, Los Angeles (79.PB.72)

159
Jennifer Angaiak Wood, *Inuit Mask of a Puffin*, 2019, alder wood, acrylic paint and feathers, 38.1 × 35.6 × 10.2 (15 × 14 × 4). © Jennifer Angaiak Wood

160
Lucian Freud, *Rotted Puffin*, 1944, Conté and coloured crayon on paper, 18.4 × 13.3 (7 ¼ × 5 ¼). Private Collection. © The Lucian Freud Archive. All Rights Reserved 2025/ Bridgeman Images

161
John Bellany, *Spes Maris*, early 1980s, oil on canvas, 213.3 × 172.7 (84 × 68). Private Collection. © Estate of John Bellany. All rights reserved 2025/Bridgeman Images

162
Artist unknown, *Loon*, wood. Photo Mark Miller/Alamy Photo Stock

164
Richard Kearton, *Black Throated Diver*, 1905, hand-coloured photogravure, 19.6 × 28.1 (7 ¾ × 11 ⅛). J. Paul Getty Museum, Los Angeles (84.XM.500.10)

165
e bond, *Common Loon*, 2021, mixed media, 18 × 18 (7 ⅛ × 7 ⅛). © e bond

167
Maker unknown, bird ornament, 600–800, shell, 6.4 × 6.4 × 1.3 (2 ½ × 2 ½ × ½). Metropolitan Museum of Art, New York. The Michael C. Rockefeller Memorial Collection, Purchase, Mrs. Gertrud A. Mellon Gift, 1963 (1978.412.103)

168, 169
Utagawa Kunisada, *Watching Cormorant Fishing from a Pleasure Boat* (*Ukaibune no asobi*), 1852, two of three panels, woodblock print, ink and colour on paper. Bridgeman Images

170
Vittore Carpaccio, *Hunting on the Lagoon* (detail), *c.* 1490–95, oil on panel, 75.6 × 63.8 (29 ⅞ × 25 ⅛). J. Paul Getty Museum, Los Angeles (79.PB.72)

171
Walter Inglis Anderson, *Dead Cormorant*, 1960–65, watercolour over graphite on off-white wove paper, 27.8 × 21.4 (11 × 8 ½). Art Institute of Chicago. Gift of family of Walter Anderson (1991.715)/Art Resource, NY/ Scala, Florence. © The Estate of the Artist

173
Maker unknown, 'St Cuthbert with Eider Ducks at his Feet', from the East Window at St Cuthbert's Church, Amble, Northumberland, late nineteenth–early twentieth century, stained-glass. Mark Sunderland Photography/Alamy Stock Photo

174–175
Bruno Liljefors, *Common Eiders on Rocky Islets*, 1897, oil on canvas, 61 × 151 (24 ⅛ × 59 ½). Private Collection. Photo Stockholms Auktionsverk

176
Jean Metzinger, *Coloured Landscape with Aquatic Birds* (detail), 1907–8, oil on canvas, 75.5 × 101 (29 ¾ × 39 ⅞). Musee d'Art Moderne de la Ville de Paris (MAM), Paris/ Bridgeman Images. © 2026 ADAGP, Paris and DACS, London

178
Lü Ji, *Mandarin Ducks and Cotton Rose Hibiscus* (detail), late fifteenth century, hanging scroll, ink and colour on silk, 172.7 × 99.1 (68 × 39). Metropolitan Museum of Art, New York. Ex coll. C. C. Wang Family, Gift of Oscar L. Tang Family, 2005 (2005.494.2)

180
Yōshū (Hashimoto) Chikanobu, *Chiyoda Castle* (Album of Women) (detail), 1895, triptych of woodblock prints, 35.2 × 23.4 (13 ⅞ × 9 ¼). Metropolitan Museum of Art, New York. Gift of Mrs. W. Walton Butterworth, 1979 (JP3557)

181
Utagawa Kuniyoshi, *Kawazu Saburô Sukeyasu as the spirit of the mandarin duck and Matano Gorô with lantern, scene from a kabuki play*, 1845–47, woodcut, 35.6 × 23.5 (14 × 9 ¼). Metropolitan Museum of Art, New York. Gift of Mary L. Cassilly, 1894 (JP206)

182
Maker unknown, relief fragment with two birds in the papyrus thicket, *c.* 1925–1900 BCE, limestone and paint, 18.5 × 25.5 × 5.5 (7 ⅜ × 10 ⅛ × 2 ¼). Metropolitan Museum of Art, New York. Rogers Fund, 1913 (13.235.9)

183
Frans Snyders, *Fable of Fox and Heron*, 1630s, oil on canvas, 121 × 238 (47 ¾ × 93 ¾). Nationalmuseum, Stockholm (NM 1486)

185
Jan Weenix, *Gamepiece with a Dead Heron*, 1695, oil on canvas, 134 × 111.1 (52 ⅞ × 43 ¾). Metropolitan Museum of Art, New York. Rogers Fund, 1950 (50.55)

187
Artist unknown, *Gray Heron (Aosagi) and Mizu-aoi Plant*, 1857, woodblock print, 35.6 × 24.4 (14 × 9 ⅝). Metropolitan Museum of Art, New York. Bequest of Grace M. Pugh, 1985 (JP3704)

189
After Hieronymus Bosch, *The Concert in the Egg* (detail), *c.* 1561, oil on canvas, 108 × 126 (42 ⅝ × 49 ⅝). Musée des Beaux-Arts, Lille (P.816). Photo Album/Alamy Stock Photo

190
Artist unknown, *Rama and Lakshmana Search in Vain for Sita*, *c.* 1680–90, ink and opaque watercolour on paper, 26 × 41.3 (10 ¼ × 16 ¼). Metropolitan Museum of Art, New York. Purchase, T. Roland Berner Fund, 1974 (1974.148)

191
Karl Muhlmeister, 'Stork', from *A Cheerful Picture Book with Old and New Rhymes* by Hans Lustig, Munich, 1900. Smithsonian Libraries and Archives

193
Paul Cézanne, *Leda and the Swan*, *c.* 1880 (possibly later), oil on canvas, 59.7 × 74.9 (23 ½ × 29 ½). The Barnes Foundation, Philadelphia (BF36)

194
After Leonardo da Vinci, *Leda and the Swan*, before 1517, tempera on panel, 115 × 86 (45 ⅜ × 33 ⅞). Galleria Borghese, Rome (434)

195
Larry Colwell, *New York City Ballet, Swan Lake*, 1944–66, photographic print. Box 6, folders 6, and Box 8, folders 8–9, Larry Colwell Dance Photographs Collection, Music Division, Library of Congress, Washington, DC.

196–197
Jan Asselijn, *The Threatened Swan*, *c.* 1650, oil on canvas, 144 × 171 (56 ¾ × 67 ⅜). Rijksmuseum, Amsterdam (SK-A-4)

198
Gerald of Wales, cranes taking it in turns to sleep, late twelfth to early thirteenth century, from *Topographia Hibernica*. British Library (Harley 4751 f.39)

200
Maker unknown, *Woman's Haori with White and Red Cranes*, 1920–40, silk. Rijksmuseum, Amsterdam. Gift of Jan Dees & René van der Star, 2009 (AK-RAK-2009-3-37)

201
Utagawa Hiroshige, 'Minowa, Kanasugi, Mikawashima', 1856–58, from the series *One Hundred Famous Views of Edo*, woodblock print, 33.7 × 21.7 (13 ¼ × 8 ⅝). Metropolitan Museum of Art, New York. Rogers Fund, 1914 (JP63)

202
Tawaraya Sōtatsu, *Anthology with Crane Design* (detail), seventeenth century, ink and colour on paper, full scroll: 34 × 1,356 (13 ½ × 533 ⅞). Kyoto National Museum (AK364)

203
Artist unknown, *Krishna Vanquishing the Crane-Demon Bakasura*, late 1700s, gum tempera and gold on paper, 27.8 × 19.7 (11 × 7 ¾). Cleveland Museum of Art. John L. Severance Fund (1966.29)

204
Neil Welliver, *Osprey's Nest*, 1979, colour woodcut on gampi paper, 75.25 × 80.01 (29 ⅝ × 31 ½). Private Collection/ Bridgeman Images. © Neil Welliver, courtesy Alexandre Gallery, New York

206
Artist unknown (Japan), *Osprey*, nineteenth century, woodblock print on paper, 18.1 × 24.3 (7 ¼ × 9 ⅝). Maidstone Museum and Art Gallery/Bridgeman Images

207
Edwin Austin Abbey, *Figure Study (woman with osprey headdress and white fur colour)*, *c.* 1871–1911, oil on canvas, 61 × 45.7 (24 × 18). Yale University Art Gallery, New Haven, CT. Edwin Austin Abbey Memorial Collection (1937.2517)

208
Sir John Tenniel, *Alice trying to play croquet with flamingo and hedgehog*, 1866, pencil drawing, 13 × 7.5 (5 × 3). Henry W. and Albert A. Berg Collection of English and American Literature, The New York Public Library (b15887349)

210
Raphaël Delorme, *Flamante Rose*, n.d., oil on canvas, 42 × 33 (16 ⅝ × 13). Photo Christie's Images/Scala, Florence. © The Artist's Estate

211
Alexander Calder, *Flamingo*, 1973, sheet metal and paint, Federal Center Plaza, Chicago. Photo DeAgostini Picture Library/Scala, Florence. © 2026 Calder Foundation, New York / DACS, London

212
Maker unknown, inlay depicting Thoth as the ibis with a maat feather, fourth century BCE, faience, 15.5 × 15.6 × 1 (6 ⅛ × 6 ¼ × ½). Metropolitan Museum of Art, New York. Purchase, Edward S. Harkness Gift, 1926 (26.7.992)

214
Leon Jean Joseph Dubois, 'Thoth twice great, presiding over the lower region', from *Egyptian Pantheon: a collection of mythological figures from ancient Egypt, based on monuments, with explanatory text*, Paris, 1823–25. General Research Division, The New York Public Library (b14073799)

215
Edgar Degas, *Young Woman with Ibis*, 1857–58, reworked 1860–62, oil on canvas, 100 × 74.9 (39 ⅜ × 29 ½). Metropolitan Museum of Art, New York. Gift of Stephen Mazoh and Purchase, Bequest of Gioconda King, by exchange, 2008 (2008.277)

216
Samuel Jessurun de Mesquita, *Egret*, 1913, print, 37.2 × 28.8 (14 ¾ × 11 ⅜). Rijksmuseum, Amsterdam (RP-P-1914-4229)

217
Michelino da Besozzo (attr.), *Madonna of the Rose Garden*, 1420–35, tempera on panel, 130 × 95 (51 × 37). Museo di Castelvecchio, Verona. Photo Scala, Florence

218
Melchior d'Hondecoeter, *The Floating Feather*, *c.* 1680, oil on canvas, 159 × 144 (62 ⅝ × 56 ¾). Rijksmuseum, Amsterdam (SK-A-175)

221
Ian Rees, *Great Blue Heron*, 2025, colour pencil on Bristol Paper © Ian Rees

INDEX

Bold page numbers indicate main illustrated entries for individual birds; *italic* numbers refer to other illustrations

To Valerie, who gives full meaning to her name: dignity and strength.

Dr Colin Rees is a scientist and naturalist who has devoted his entire career to the conservation of the natural environment. He has worked for various international organizations that have enabled him to appreciate the extraordinary diversity of life and cultures around the world. His books include *Birds of the Philippines*, *Birds of a Feather: Seasonal Changes on Both Sides of the Atlantic*, *A History of Cornish Ornithology*, *The Path to Conservation* and *Nature's Calendar: A Year in the Life of a Wildlife Sanctuary*. He regularly contributes to journals and magazines.

Front cover: Utagawa Hiroshige, 'Minowa, Kanasugi, Mikawashima' (detail of p. 201), 1856–58, from the series *One Hundred Famous Views of Edo*, woodblock print, 33.7 × 21.7 cm (13 ¼ × 8 ⅝ in.). Metropolitan Museum of Art, New York. Rogers Fund, 1914 (JP63). Photo LMA/AW/Alamy Stock Photo.

Spine (top to bottom): John James Audubon, 'Whooping Crane, Male, adult', no. 63, pl. 313 (detail of p. 199), 1842, from *The Birds of America*, vol. V. Philadelphia, 1842. General Research Division, The New York Public Library (b13559627); King Eider (*Somateria spectabilis*), from *Illustrations of British Birds* by H. L. Meyer, vol. 4, London, 1837. Smithsonian Libraries and Archives; Heron (*Ardea cinerea*) from *Coloured Illustrations of British Birds, and Their Eggs* by H. L. Meyer, vol. 4, London, 1842. Smithsonian Libraries and Archives; Night Heron (*Adrea mycticorax*) from *Coloured Illustrations of British Birds, and Their Eggs* by H. L. Meyer, vol. 4, London, 1842. Smithsonian Libraries and Archives; Puffin (*Fratercula arctica*), from *Illustrations of British Birds* by H. L. Meyer, vol. 4, London, 1837. Smithsonian Libraries and Archives.

Back cover: Maker unknown, *Woman's Haori with White and Red Cranes* (details of p. 200), 1920–40, silk. Rijksmuseum, Amsterdam. Gift of Jan Dees & René van der Star, 2009 (AK-RAK-2009-3-37).

First published in the United Kingdom in 2026 by Thames & Hudson Ltd, 6–24 Britannia Street, London WC1X 9JD

EU Authorized Representative:
Interart S.A.R.L.
19 rue Charles Auray,
93500 Pantin, Paris, France
productsafety@thameshudson.co.uk
interart.fr

A CIP catalogue record for this book is available from the British Library

ISBN 978-0-500-02926-8
01

Printed and bound in China by C&C Offset Printing Co. Ltd.

MIX
Paper | Supporting responsible forestry
FSC® C008047
www.fsc.org